A Longing for the Light

A Longing for the Light

SELECTED POEMS OF

Vicente Aleixandre

Edited by Lewis Hyde

Copper Canyon Press
Port Townsend, Washington

Cover art: Carolyn Watts, *Hai,* 2004. Charcoal and pastel on paper, 9" x 9".

Copper Canyon Press is in residence at Fort Worden State Park in Port Townsend, Washington, under the auspices of Centrum, a gathering place for artists and creative thinkers from around the world, students of all ages and backgrounds, and audiences seeking extraordinary cultural enrichment.

LIBRARY OF CONGRESS CATALOGING-IN-PUBLICATION DATA
Aleixandre, Vicente, 1898–1984.
[Poems. English. Selections]
A longing for the light : selected poems of Vicente Aleixandre / edited by Lewis Hyde.—2nd ed.
p. cm.
Includes bibliographical references and indexes.
ISBN 978-1-55659-254-6 (pbk. : alk. paper)
1. Aleixandre, Vicente, 1898-1984—Translations into English.
I. Hyde, Lewis, 1945- II. Title.

PQ6601.L26A23 2007
861'.62—dc22

2007000992

Second edition

COPPER CANYON PRESS
Post Office Box 271
Port Townsend, Washington 98368
www.coppercanyonpress.org

TRANSLATED FROM THE SPANISH BY

Lewis Hyde, Stephen Kessler, Robert Bly, David Pritchard, David Unger

AND

Pilar Zalamea, Allen Kimbrell, Deborah Weinberger, Geoffrey Rips,
Willis Barnstone, David Garrison, Timothy Baland, Shepherd Bliss,
W.S. Merwin, Tomás O'Leary

Contents

PROSE INTERLUDE

Poems with White Light

RECENT POEMS

INDEXES

INTRODUCTION

I

People feel different kinds of loneliness. There is the loneliness of boredom or of being without friends. For some people there is the loneliness of feeling separated from the whole world, from the physical world in particular, the trees, the grass, the places where fish hide under water, and the moon. Camus felt how "strangeness creeps in: perceiving that the world is 'dense,' sensing to what a degree a stone is foreign and irreducible to us, with what intensity nature or a landscape can make us into nothing. At the heart of all beauty lies something inhuman, and these hills, the softness of the sky, the outline of these trees at this very minute lose the illusory meaning we had dressed them in, henceforth more remote than a lost paradise."

This feeling is neutral. Some find it a source of joy, saying that the world is all the more a gift because it has so little to do with us. Others take it as a sadness, not out of philosophy but just because that's how it meets them every day, every time the mind comes to rest.

Vicente Aleixandre's early poems—for almost twenty years—were fed by the sadness. There are love poems and there are poems with a sort of surrealist wit, but the sadness runs beneath all of them. "The moon comes out and chases what used to be a man's bones..." The loneliness, the kind we usually associate with exiles, keeps coming back, overflowing from the poet's body and contaminating the rest of his life.

And all around the emptiness is that moon, or the light or the sea, all those things that move with such grace that we feel awkward. There must have been a time when we were part of it. We must have been born to be one of those pure elements, "a chip of light, to burn itself up / with love-making." But everywhere you look there is a world of manners and dress clothes and self-consciousness. You can feel it—the lost paradise—but it's a thing that isn't there. Aleixandre always spoke of it with a backward style that a friend of his called "almost affirmative negation." The world that's gone is given and taken away in one phrase. He doesn't say that his lover's breath shakes the leaves. He wishes he could say that, but he can't; he has to tell us about "the air that doesn't move any leaves that aren't green."

Aleixandre keeps seeing two things that won't come together. As you go through these poems you will find them filled with edges, limits, shorelines, and boundaries that can't be crossed. The poems are often set by the sea, as if pulled toward the energy that's trapped in pools along the shoreline, the line no one may step over:

> You must never mix blood with such free waves.
> The color white is wing, is water, is cloud, is sail;
> but it's never a face...

There is a way to cross over. There is an energy that runs throughout the universe and makes it whole, and we can enter it through love or through any of the forces that break things down—death, anger, hate, poetry, stripping off clothes, getting down on all fours with the animals—anything that obliterates reflective consciousness.

Aleixandre didn't consider himself a strict surrealist, but there are certain affinities. The surrealists share his distrust of the logical mind and his fascination with the sea. Aleixandre described the poet the same way the surrealists did, as someone who speaks for the earth with forces that rise through the soles of his feet. Freud's work connects them also. André Breton read Freud just before he wrote the first Manifesto of Surrealism in 1924. Aleixandre read him in 1928 and readily declares the influence on his early work. From Freud, from dreams, from the voices that come just before sleep, these poets knew there was an interior world different from a stock exchange or a street map of Madrid. It pulled them powerfully. It's as if they were in a strong undertow beneath the accelerating tide of rationalism. The anthropologist in the jungle, the Spanish painters, the French poets, the psychoanalysts were all down there, pushed slowly backward by the energy of the current above them.

But they were not yet in touch with that other world in a nourishing way. (Only when you are moving away from the "realistic attitude" do you find melted clocks; when you have actually left it there aren't any clocks at all.) The forces they were entering were only dimly perceived, like the shapes of fish seen deep under water. No one knew what it meant to go down there. Perhaps if they honored this new thing they would have to abandon or destroy the old. Perhaps this new world, forgotten since the "Enlightenment," would be weak or unhuman. And if it were the opposite of drawing room decorum it might well rip someone to pieces. Whatever the reason, there always seems to be a fog of tension and blood around those early surrealist poems. The Nature that Aleixandre sees across the edge of his human eye is not a gentle one: it is full of breaking waves and lightning and growls. Nor is there much solace in the longed-for erotic life, for a fear of the lover, a fear of being truly consumed by passion, lies in the shadow of desire:

> Don't come any closer. Your glowing face, live coal that stirs my
> consciousness,
> the shining pain where all of a sudden I'm tempted to die,
> to burn my lips on your indelible friction,
> to feel my flesh melting, embraced in your burning diamond.

The poems are not an affirmation. They are not working out of a full and nourishing surreality, but away from the reality at hand. That too is part of their tension—they are the reflective mind trying to think its way out of coherence and precision. Nothing from the social world can be trusted. The poems try to break themselves down, like a child who tries to become invisible when he discovers his parents have no interest in him. They are hard to examine closely. The images won't stick together, the syntax breaks, the plot shifts, the objects shine and fade, the proportions of things seem odd. It's as if you have to find the correct place to stand and observe them. If you come too close they seem shaggy and unkempt like the animals in Aleixandre's jungle: "lions like a heart covered with hair…, / the yellow hyena who disguises himself as the greedy, greedy sunset." But when you back off and watch from a distance, they're still hard to focus on, as if the jungle were now covered with steam.

It may be a matter of finding the right light. Aleixandre wrote that the poems are best understood when seen in "rainbow light." He often described his work as *una aspiración a la luz,* a longing for the light. The earliest poems, he said, were lit with black light, as if he'd been dragged far under the sea where nothing could penetrate, where the fish must attract each other with their own luminescence. Then he began to rise. By the fourth book, *Destruction or Love,*[1] a light can be seen in the distance but it has traveled so far through the water that it's red when it arrives. But he keeps rising. *The Shadow of Paradise,* he says, is "a song for the dawn of the world, a hymn sung for light from the knowledge of darkness." His backward style is a way of writing in this half-light.

It is important that he found a way to keep writing, for Aleixandre is one of the few pessimistic poets of the twentieth century who managed to rise and find something above the emptiness. The shift was fairly dramatic. It came with *The Story of the Heart* (1954). Aleixandre does not lose his gloominess in this book, but despair becomes only one of the tones his voice can take, a part of the register, not the whole song. The bulk of the book affirms human fellowship, a spiritual unity, friendliness. He has written that it "was begun as a work of love in the strict sense." From there it opens outward to a world of people. It makes his early books seem almost reticent. The poems are social, the style is

---

1. The *or* in Aleixandre's work usually reads as an equal sign: Destruction = Love.

narrative, almost talky. There are real people all around and he pays attention to them, to friends and lovers, to strangers and dead heroes, to his dog. Aleixandre himself appears more and more in the poems.

Whereas before his imagination flourished in a kind of dream time—and that sort of time is oddly dissociated from human things—now the poems turn to the historical world, to daily time, the passing of real events, sequences in which love is not quite the same as death, for one precedes the other. And whereas before Aleixandre had been attentive to nature out of a nostalgic longing to join it, now nature is just the background for the lives of human beings. In the introduction to his selected poems he wrote, "This now is the opposite of human loneliness. No, we aren't alone."

II

Vicente Aleixandre is not a poet whose life was particularly instructive of the poetry. He was born in 1898 in Seville, where his grandfather was regional military commander. His father was an engineer. During most of his childhood the family lived in Málaga on the Mediterranean coast just southeast of Seville. It would seem that as he grew up Aleixandre had two careers. The one, an informal and hidden attention to literature, grew quietly beneath the other more formal and public life. In college he studied law and business administration. By the time he was twenty-two he was teaching business law in Madrid and helping to edit an economics review. At one point a railway company hired him, and his first published pieces were some articles about trains.

He spent the summer of 1917, when he was nineteen, in a small town in the mountains. There a friend gave him a book of poems by Rubén Darío. Until that time he had read widely, but mostly nineteenth-century novels, not poetry. That summer, after Darío struck, he read Antonio Machado and Juan Ramón Jiménez. And he began to write. But always in secret, as if it were just a pastime. Carlos Bousoño, who wrote the best early book on Aleixandre, says that in those years "not even his closest friends knew the secret, passionate work Aleixandre gave himself to in his uneasy solitude." He still taught law; he was reading the Spanish mystics when he wrote those railway articles. This went on for eight years. Finally, when he was twenty-seven, he collapsed with an illness that forced him, or allowed him, to abandon his job and spend two years "inactive" in the mountains. Almost immediately he began to publish poems, and within three years his first book appeared. He was ill again several times during the 1930s, including a long convalescence that isolated him during the Spanish Civil War. He was one of the few Spanish poets who was able both to survive the war and to remain in Spain. He never had been a political poet.

His first book after the war established him as a guiding force among Spain's younger poets, their link to the past. When, in 1968, the publishing house Insula came to issue a volume honoring Aleixandre, they could include poems from García Lorca, Pablo Neruda, Rafael Alberti, Gerardo Diego, Miguel Hernández, Blas de Otero, and more than seventy other Spanish poets.

Aleixandre died at his home in Madrid in December 1984 at the age of 86.

III

A book of this kind is the work of many hands. And though only one name appears on most translations, few are the work of only one imagination. Particular thanks must go to Robert Bly, who not only first introduced me to Aleixandre's work but also went on to share with me his discoveries in the art of translation and to help me re-imagine many more of the poems in this book than the few that bear his name. José Olivio Jiménez helped me widen my selection of poems and guided me though Aleixandre's prose. Most invaluable, Hardie St. Martin tirelessly read the work in both languages and, with his sharp blue pencil, saved me from error, highlighted subtleties in the Spanish, and discovered remarkable solutions to nearly insoluble dilemmas.

Finally, of course, my gratitude to Vicente Aleixandre, who helped me with the initial selection of poems, who patiently answered my questions over the years, and who gave all of us the real gift, the poetry.

Early Poems

CERRADA

Campo desnudo. Sola
la noche inerme. El viento
insinúa latidos
sordos contra sus lienzos.

La sombra a plomo ciñe,
fría, sobre tu seno
su seda grave, negra,
cerrada. Queda opreso

el bulto así en materia
de noche, insigne, quieto
sobre el límpido plano
retrasado del cielo.

Hay estrellas fallidas.
Pulidos goznes. Hielos
flotan a la deriva
en lo alto. Fríos lentos.

Una sombra que pasa,
sobre el contorno serio
y mudo bate, adusta,
su látigo secreto.

Flagelación. Corales
de sangre o luz o fuego
bajo el cendal se auguran,
vetean, ceden luego.

Closed

Bare earth. The defenseless
night alone. The wind
insinuates deaf throbbings
against its draperies.

The shadow of lead,
cold, wraps your breast
in its heavy silk, black,
closed. So the mass

is pressed down by the material
of night, famous, quiet,
over the limpid
late plane of night.

There are bankrupt stars.
Polished hinges. Ice
drifts along
in the heights. Slow streams of cold.

A shadow passing
over the mute grave contour
lashes, austere,
its secret whip.

Flagellation. Corals
of blood or light or fire
are divined under the gauze,
grow mottled, then give way.

O carne o luz de carne,
profunda. Vive el viento
porque anticipa ráfagas,
cruces, pausas, silencios.

FROM *ÁMBITO*

Either flesh or the light of flesh,
deep. The wind lives
because it looks forward to gusts,
cross-currents, pauses, silences.

TRANSLATED BY W.S. MERWIN

MAR Y AURORA

Descubiertas las ondas velan
todavía sin sol, prematinales.
Afilados asoman por oriente
sonrosados atrevimientos del día.
Las largas lenguas palpan
las pesadas aguas, la tensa
lámina de metal,
aún fría y bronca al roce insinuante.
Todavía emergiendo de la noche
la lisa plancha asume
adusta las comprobaciones iluminadas.
Penetran, de carne, de día,
los lentos palpos, que adoptan
ondas tímidas, pasivas espumas
bajo sus cóncavos avances.

Todo el ámbito se recorre, se llena
de crecientes tentáculos,
alba clara, alba fina, que se adentra
a volúmenes largos, en estratos de luz,
desalojando la estéril sombra,
fácil presa a esta hora.
Comienzan a alzarse bultos
de espuma voluntaria,
inminentes.
No permitáis que emerja.
Hinche el agua la redonda
sospecha, y se adivine
el día abajo, pujante bajo el manto
líquido, poderoso a alzarse

SEA AND SUNRISE

Before sunrise, still in darkness,
the uncovered waves keep watch.
In the east, the day begins to lift
its sharp and timid advances.
Long tongues feel their way
over the heavy water, the taut
metallic plate,
cold and rough to that soft stroking.
Still emerging from the night,
the smooth sheet rises up
and displays its illuminated proofs.
By day, by flesh, the slow
feelers push in, taking over
the shy, passive whitecaps
beneath their curving progress.

The whole area is covered, filled
with lengthening tentacles,
clear dawn, thin dawn that penetrates
long spaces, layers of light,
pushing out the barren shadow,
an easy prey at this hour.
Lumps of imminent,
willing
foam begin to build up.
Don't let it come out!
Let the water raise the round
possibility, let the day be seen
below, pushing under the liquid
mantle, strong enough to rise

con el mar, abismo cancelable.
La luz venga del hondo,
rota en cristales de agua,
destellos de clamores
disueltos—no: resueltos—
sin torpe algarabía.
Surta en abiertas miras
con orden y se adueñe
del esqueleto oscuro
del aire y lo desarme,
y limpio espacio brille
—sometido a su dueño—,
lento, diario, culto
bebedor de las ondas.

FROM *ÁMBITO*

with the sea, that temporary abyss.
Let the light come from the deep,
broken into crystals of water,
flashes of dissolved—no:
resolved—outcries
that have no dull jabber.
Let it gush in on target,
in order, let it capture
and disarm the air's
dark skeleton,
and let the clean space shine
in the hands of its captor—
the slow, elegant, daily
drinker of the waves.

TRANSLATED BY DAVID UNGER AND LEWIS HYDE

MAR Y NOCHE

El mar bituminoso aplasta sombras
contra si mismo. Oquedades de azules
profundos quedan quietas al arco de las ondas.
Voluta ancha de acero quedaría
de súbito forjada si el instante
siguiente no derribase la alta fábrica.
Tumultos, cataclismos de volúmenes
irrumpen de lo alto a la ancha base,
que se deshace ronca,
tragadora de sí y del tiempo, contra el aire
mural, torpe al empuje.
Bajo cielos altísimos y negros
muge—clamor—la honda
boca, y pide noche.
Boca—mar—toda ella, pide noche;
noche extensa, bien prieta y grande,
para sus fauces hórridas, y enseña
todos sus blancos dientes de espuma.
Una pirámide linguada
de masa torva y fría
se alza, pide,
se hunde luego en la cóncava garganta
y tiembla abajo, presta otra
vez a levantarse, voraz de la alta noche,
que rueda por los cielos
—redonda, pura, oscura, ajena—
dulce en la serenidad del espacio.

Se debaten las fuerzas inútiles abajo.
Torso y miembros. Las duras

SEA AND NIGHT

The bituminous sea crushes shadows
against itself. Deep blue hollows
hang in the arch of the waves.
The wide whorl of steel forged suddenly
would last, if the next moment
didn't tear down its tower.
Tumultuous catastrophic volumes
crash down into the wide foundation
that roars as it comes apart,
swallowing both itself and time
in a clumsy assault on the wall of air.
Under a distant, blackened sky
the deep mouth roars—cries out—
and begs for night.
Mouth—sea—all of it pleads for night,
vast night, pitch black and huge,
pleads with its horrid throats, baring
all its white foam teeth.
A pyramid of tongues,
cold, grim, massive,
lifts up and pleads,
then drowns itself in the concave throat
and, trembling below, readies itself
to rise again, hungry for the distant night
that rolls across the sky—
round, pure, dark, remote—
sweet in the peace of space.

The helpless forces struggle deep below.
Torso and limbs, the taut

contracciones enseñan
músculos emergidos, redondos bultos,
álgidos despidos.
Parece atado al hondo
abismo el mar, en cruz, mirando
al cielo alto, por desasirse,
violento, rugiente, clavado al lecho negro.

Mientras la noche rueda
en paz, graciosa, bella,
en ligado desliz, sin rayar nada
el espacio, capaz de órbita y comba
firmes, hasta hundirse en la dulce
claridad ya lechosa,
mullida grama donde
cesar, reluciente de roces secretos,
pulida, brilladora,
maestro en superficie.

FROM *ÁMBITO*

contractions reveal
the emerging muscles, round bulges,
freezing spray.
The sea seems bound
to the deep abyss, crucified, staring
at the high heavens, about to escape,
violent, bellowing, nailed to its black bed.

Meanwhile, the night orbits
in peace, graceful, lovely,
having slipped her moorings, leaving the space
unmarked, able to orbit, to curve firmly,
until she sinks into the sweet
clarity now pearling,
the cushion of grasses where
she will fall, gleaming from mysterious strokings,
polished, glittering,
mistress of surfaces.

TRANSLATED BY PILAR ZALAMEA AND ALLEN KIMBRELL

Iban entrando uno a uno y las paredes desangradas no eran de marmol frío. Entraban innumerables y se saludaban con los sombreros. Demonios de corta vista visitaban los corazones. Se miraban con desconfianza. Estropajos yacían sobre los suelos y las avispas los ignoraban. Un sabor a tierra reseca descargaba de pronto sobre las lenguas y se hablaba de todo con conocimiento. Aquella dama, aquella señora argumentaba con su sombrero y los pechos de todos se hundían muy lentamente. Aguas. Naufragio. Equilibrio de las miradas. El cielo permanecía a su nivel, y un humo de lejanía salvaba todos las cosas. Los dedos de la mano del más viejo tenían tanta tristeza que el pasillo se acercaba lentamente, a la deriva, recargado de historias. Todos pasaban íntegramente a sí mismos y un telón de humo se hacía sangre todo. Sin remediarlo, las camisas temblaban bajo las chaquetas y las marcas de ropa estaban bordadas sobre la carne. "¿Me amas, di?" La más joven sonreía llena de anuncios. Brisas, brisas de abajo resolvían toda la niebla, y ella quedaba desnuda, irisada de acentos, hecha pura prosodia. "Te amo, sí" —y las paredes delicuescentes casi se deshacían en vaho. "Te amo, sí, temblorosa, aunque te deshagas como un helado." La abrazó como a música. Le silbaban los oídos. Ecos, sueños de melodía se detenían, vacilaban en las gargantas como un agua muy triste. "Tienes los ojos tan claros que se te transparentan los sesos." Una lágrima. Moscas blancas bordoneaban sin entusiasmo. La luz de percal barato se amontonaba por los rincones. Todos los señoras sentados sobre sus inocencias bostezaban sin desconfianza. El amor es una razón de Estado. Nos hacemos cargo de que los besos no son de *biscuit glacé*. Pero si ahora se abriese esa puerta todos nos besaríamos en la boca. ¡Qué asco que el mundo no gire sobre sus goznes! Voy a dar media vuelta a mis penas para que los canarios flautas puedan amarme. Ellos, los amantes, faltaban a su deber y se fatigaban como los pàjaros. Sobre las sillas las formas no son de metal. Te beso, pero tus pestañas… Las agujas del aire estaban sobre las frentes:

DEATH OR THE WAITING ROOM

They went in one by one and the walls had been drained of blood and were not made of cold marble. Countless numbers were going in, greeting each other with a tip of the hat. Nearsighted demons came to check on their hearts. They watched each other suspiciously. Mops lay on the floor and the wasps didn't notice. All of a sudden the taste of dried-out dirt broke over their tongues and they talked about everything with cleverness. That woman, that lady there got into an argument with her hat and everybody's breasts began to sink very slowly. Water. Shipwreck. A balance of glances. The sky stayed at its proper level and a smoke from the distance saved everything. The fingers of the oldest man's hand were so sad that the corridor drifted slowly over to him, full of stories to tell. The whole group passed ahead of itself and a curtain of smoke turned completely to blood. Without doing anything about it, the shirts were trembling under their jackets and the shirt labels were embroidered on flesh. "Tell me, do you love me?" The youngest girl smiled, full of advertising. The wind, a little wind from beneath dissolved the mist and she was left naked, made into pure prosody, iridescent with accents. "Yes, I love you"—and the soggy walls nearly turned into steam. "I love you, yes, O Shivering One, even though you're melting like an ice cream cone." He hugged her like music. It made his ears whistle. The echoes, the tunes from a dream, were held there, hesitating in their throats like a very sad water. "Your eyes are so clear that your brains shine right through." A teardrop. White flies wandered around without enthusiasm. The light was piled up in the corners like cheap percale. All the gentlemen, sure of themselves, yawned as they sat on their innocence. Love is Government business. We fully realize that kisses aren't made of baked Alaska. But if that door were to open now we'd all kiss each other on the mouth. What a shame that the world doesn't swing on its hinges! I'm going to turn my troubles halfway around so the canaries will be able to love me. They, the lovers, didn't do what they should have done and got

qué oscura misión la mìa de amarte. Las paredes de nìquel no consentían el crepúsculo, lo devolvían herido. Los amantes volaban masticando la luz. Permíteme que te diga. Las viejas contaban muertes, muertes y respiraban por sus encajes. Las barbas de los demás crecían hacia el espanto: la hora final las segará sin dolor. Abanicos de tela paraban acariciaban escrúpulos. Ternura de presentirse horizontal. Fronteras.

La hora grande se acercaba en la bruma. La sala cabeceaba sobre el mar de cáscaras de naranja. Remaríamos sin entrañas si los pulsos no estuvieran en las muñecas. El mar es amargo. Tu beso me ha sentado mal al estómago. Se acerca la hora.

La puerta, presta a abrirse, se teñía de amarillo lóbrego lamentándose de su torpeza. Dónde encontrarte, oh sentido de la vida, si ya no hay tiempo. Todos los seres esperaban la voz de Jehová refulgente de metal blanco. Los amantes se besaban sobre los nombres. Los pañuelos eran narcóticos y restañaban la carne exangüe. Las siete y diez. La puerta volaba sin plumas y el ángel del Señor anunció a María. Puede pasar el primero.

FROM PASÍON DE LA TIERRA

16

tired like the birds. The shapes on the chairs aren't made of metal. I kiss you, but your eyelashes … The airborne needles were over the foreheads: I have such a dark mission, loving you. The nickel walls didn't accept the twilight so they sent it back, wounded. The lovers flew about chewing the light. Allow me to tell you. The old ladies counted up the casualties, the casualties and they breathed through their lace. Everyone else's beard grew down toward horror: the final hour will mow them down painlessly. The woven fans wavered, toying with their scrupulousness. How touching to see yourself laid out ahead of time. Boundaries.

The great hour was coming closer through the fog. The room bobbed on the sea of orange peels. We could row gutlessly if it weren't for the heartbeats in our wrists. The sea is bitter. Your kiss gave me an upset stomach. The hour is near.

The door—the one about to open—had turned a mournful yellow because it felt so heavy. Where will you be found, O Meaning of Life, when there isn't any time left. Everybody waited for Jehovah's gleaming white metal voice. The lovers kissed each other's names. The narcotic handkerchiefs sopped up the bloodless flesh. Ten after seven. The door flew up without any feathers and the Angel of the Lord announced Mary. Whoever's first may come in now.

Translated by Lewis Hyde

Esa luz amarilla que la luna me envía es una historia larga que me acongoja más que un brazo desnudo. ¿Por qué me tocas, si sabes que no puedo responderte? ¿Por qué insistes nuevamente, si sabes que contra tu azul profundo, casi líquido, no puedo más que cerrar los ojos, ignorar las aguas muertas, no oír las músicas sordas de los peces de arriba, olvidar la forma de su cuadrado estanque? ¿Por qué abres tu boca reciente, para que yo sienta sobre mi cabeza que la noche no ama más que mi esperanza, porque espera verla convertida en deseo? ¿Por qué el negror de los brazos quiere tocarme el pecho y me pregunta por la nota de mi bella caja escondida, por esa cristalina palidez que se sucede siempre cuando un piano se ahoga, o cuando se escucha la extinguida nota del beso? Algo que es como un arpa que se hunde.

Pero tú, hermosísima, no quieres conocer este azul frío de que estoy revestido y besas la helada contracción de mi esfuerzo. Estoy quieto como el arco tirante, y todo para ignorarte, oh noche de los espacios cardinales, de los torrentes de silencio y de lava. ¡Si tú vieras qué esfuerzo me cuesta guardar el equilibrio contra la opresión de tu seno, contra ese martillo de hierro que me está golpeando aquí, en el séptimo espacio intercostal, preguntándome por el contacto de dos epidermis! Lo ignoro todo. No quiero saber si el color rojo es antes o es después, si Dios lo sacó de su frente o si nació del pecho del primer hombre herido. No quiero saber si los labios son una larga línea blanca.

De nada me servirá ignorar la hora que es, no tener noción de la lucha cruel, de la aurora que me está naciendo entre mi sangre. Acabaré pronunciando unas palabras relucientes. Acabaré destellando entre los dientes tu muerte prometida, tu marmórea memoria, tu torso derribado, mientras me elevo con mi sueño hasta el amanecer radiante, hasta la certidumbre germinante que me cosquillea en los ojos, entre los

SILENCE

That yellow light the moon sends down to me is a long story that troubles me more severely than a naked arm. Why do you touch me when you know I can't respond? Why do you keep insisting when you know I can do no more against your deep, almost fluid blue than close my eyes, ignore the dead waters, not hear the deaf music of the fish overhead, forget the shape of the sky's squared-off pond? Why do you open your recent mouth so I can feel on my head that the night loves nothing but my hope, the hope it wants to see turned to desire? Why does the blackness of your arms want to touch my chest and ask me for the sound of my handsome hidden box, for that glassy paleness that follows itself whenever a piano drowns, or when one hears the muffled note of a kiss? Something like a sinking harp.

But you, the most beautiful of all, don't want to get close to this cold blue I'm dressed in and you kiss the frozen contraction of my strength. I'm as quiet as a taut bow, and all for the sake of ignoring you, O night of cardinal spaces, of torrential silence and lava. If you could see what strength it takes for me to keep my balance against the pressure of your breast, against the steel hammer that hits me here, in the seventh intercostal space, asking me for the contact of two skins! I deny everything. I don't want to know if the color red comes first or last, if it was torn from the forehead of God or born from the chest of the first wounded man. I don't want to know if your lips are a long white line.

It's useless for me to forget how late it is, to have no idea of how cruel the struggle is, of the dawn now being born inside my blood. I'll end up saying a few bright words. I'll end up with your promised death, your marble memory, your knocked-down torso flashing between my teeth, while I rise with my dream to the shining dawn, to the budding certainty

párpados, prometiéndoos a todos un mundo iluminado en cuanto yo
me despierte.

Te beso, oh, pretérita, mientras miro el río en que te vas copiando, por
último, el color azul de mi frente.

FROM *PASIÓN DE LA TIERRA*

that teases my eyes, between the eyelids, promising all of you an illuminated world as soon as I wake up.

I kiss you, O thing of the past, while I watch the river where you go by, reflecting for the last time the blue color of my face.

Translated by Stephen Kessler and Lewis Hyde

Hemos mentido. Hemos una y otra vez mentido siempre. Cuando hemos caído de espalda sobre una extorsión de luz, sobre un fuego de lana burda mal parada de sueño. Cuando hemos abierto los ojos y preguntado qué tal mañana hacía. Cuando hemos estrechado la cintura, besado aquel pecho y, vuelta la cabeza, hemos adorado el plomo de una tarde muy triste. Cuando por primera vez hemos desconocido el rojo de los labios.

Todo es mentira. Soy mentira yo mismo, que me yergo a caballo en un naipe de broma y que juro que la pluma, esta gallardía que flota en mis vientos del Norte, es una sequedad que abrillanta los dientes, que pulimenta las encías. Es mentira que yo te ame. Es mentira que yo te odie. Es mentira que yo tenga la baraja entera y que el abanico de fuerza respete al abrirse el color de mis ojos.

¡Qué hambre de poder! ¡Qué hambre de locuacidad y de fuerza abofeteando duramente esta silenciosa caída de la tarde, que opone la mejilla más pálida, como disimulando la muerte que se anuncia, como evocando un cuento para dormir! ¡No quiero! ¡No tengo sueño! Tengo hartura de sorderas y de luces, de tristes acordeones secundarios y de raptos de madera para acabar con las institutrices. Tengo miedo de quedarme con la cabeza colgando sobre el pecho como una gota y que la sequedad del cielo me decapite definitivamente. Tengo miedo de evaporarme como un colchón de nubes, como una risa lateral que desgarra el lóbulo de la oreja. Tengo pánico a no ser, a que tú me golpees: "¡Eh, tú, Fulano!", y yo te responda tosiendo, cantando, señalando con el índice, con el pulgar, con el meñique, los cuatro horizontes que no me tocan (que me dardean), que me repiten en redondo.

Tengo miedo, escucha, escucha, que una mujer, una sombra, una pala, me recoja muy negra, muy de terciopelo y de acero caído, y me diga: "Te

FLYING FUGUE ON A HORSE

We've lied. Time and again we've always lied. When we fell backwards into an overcharge of light, into a fire of coarse wool slowed down with sleep. When we opened our eyes and asked what kind of day it was. When we held her by the waist, and kissed that breast and, turning our head, worshipped the lead of the saddest afternoon. When for the first time we didn't remember the redness of her lips.

Everything's a lie. I myself am a lie, mounting the horse on a joker and swearing that my plume, this elegance that floats on my north winds, is a dryness that brightens my teeth, that polishes my gums. It's a lie that I love you. It's a lie that I hate you. It's a lie that I'm playing with a full deck and that the opening fan is forced to respect the color of my eyes.

What hunger for power! What hunger for running off at the mouth and for brute force slapping this afternoon's silent decline, which turns its palest cheek, as if faking the death which is announcing itself, as if it were calling for a bedtime story! I don't want to! I'm not sleepy! I'm fed up with deafnesses and lights, with sad second accordions and wooden raptures that wipe out schoolteachers. I'm scared of getting stuck with my head hanging on my chest like a drop and that the sky's dryness will decapitate me for keeps. I'm scared of evaporating like a mattress of clouds, like a sidelong sneer that rips an earlobe. I'm in a panic that I might not be, that you'll slap me: "Hey you, Jack!" and I'll answer coughing, singing, pointing with my forefinger, my thumb, my pinkie, to the four horizons that don't touch me (but throw darts at me), that repeat me in the round.

I'm scared—listen, listen—that a woman, a shadow, a shovel, will gather me into her blackness, so velvety, so disarming, and will say: "I name

nombro. Te nombro y te hago. Tu venzo y te lanzo." Y alzando sus ojos con un viaje de brazos y un envío de tierra, me deje arriba, clavado en la punta del berbiquí más burlón, ese taladrante resquemor que me corroe los ojos, abatiéndome sobre los hombros todas las lástimas de mi garganta. Esa bisbiseante punta brillante que ha horadado el azul más ingenuo para que la carne inocente quede expuesta a la rechifla de los corazones de badana, a esos fumadores empedernidos que no saben que la sangre gotea como el humo.

¡Ah, pero no será! ¡Caballo de copas! ¡Caballo de espadas! ¡Caballo de bastos! ¡Huyamos! Alcancemos el escalón de los trapos, ese castillo exterior que malvende las caricias más lentas, que besa los pies borrando las huellas del camino. ¡Tomadme en vuestros lomos, espadas del instante, burbuja de naipe, descarriada carta sobre la mesa! ¡Tomadme! Envolvedme en la capa más roja, en ese vuelo de vuestros tendones, y conducideme a otro reino, a la heroica capacidad de amar, a la bella guarda de todas las cajas, a los dados silvestres que se sienten en los dedos tristísimos cuando las rosas naufragan junto al puente tendido de la salvación. Cuando ya no hay remedio.

Si me muero, dejadme. No me cantéis. Enterradme envuelto en la baraja que dejo, en ese bello tesoro que sabrá pulsarme como una mano imponente. Sonaré como un perfume del fondo, muy grave. Me levantaré hasta los oídos, y desde allí, hecho pura vegetación me desmentiré a mí mismo, deshachiendo mi historia, mi trazado, hasta dar en la boca entreabierta, en el Sueño que sorbe sin límites y que, como una careta de cartón, me tragará sin toserse.

From Pasión de la tierra

you. I name you and I create you. I conquer you and toss you around."
And raising her eyes, shipping me with her arms and a load of dirt, she'll
leave me up there, stuck on the point of a smart-ass drill bit, which
stings as it penetrates and eats away my eyes, loading all the sobs in my
throat up on to my shoulders. That buzzing dazzling point that pierced
the simplest blue so that innocent flesh remains exposed to the hooting
of sheepskin hearts, those hardened smokers who don't know that blood
drips just like smoke.

Ah, but it can't be! Horse of cups! Horse of swords! Horse of clubs! Let's
get out of here! We'll climb the ladder of rags, that outdoor castle where
the slowest caresses are sold at a loss, where our feet will be kissed and
the tracks of the road rubbed out. Take me on your back, swords of the
moment, card-bubble, misleading letter on the tabletop! Take me away!
Wrap me up in the reddest cloak, in that flight of your tendons, and lead
me into another kingdom, into the heroic ability to love, into the com-
bination to every safe, into the wild dice you feel in your sad fingers
when roses shipwreck next to the bridge of salvation. When there's noth-
ing you can do.

If I die, leave me alone. Don't sing to me. Bury me wrapped in the deck
I leave behind, in that lovely treasure that will know how to strum me
like a sure hand. I'll sound like a fragrance from the depths, very grave.
I'll rise to your ears, and from there, turned into pure vegetation, I'll
debunk myself, untelling my own story, my own plot, flowing back into
my mouth left ajar, into the Dream that keeps on swallowing and, like a
cardboard mask, won't cough me up.

Translated by Stephen Kessler

Poems with Red Light

Mi voz

He nacido una noche de verano
entre dos pausas. Háblame: te escucho.
He nacido. Si vieras qué agonía
representa la luna sin esfuerzo.
He nacido. Tu nombre era la dicha;
bajo un fulgor una esperanza, un ave.
Llegar, llegar. El mar era un latido,
el hueco de una mano, una medalla tibia.
Entonces son posibles ya las luces, las caricias, la piel, el horizonte,
ese decir palabras sin sentido
que ruedan como oídos, caracoles,
como un lóbulo abierto que amanece
(escucha, escucha) entre la luz pisada.

FROM *ESPADAS COMO LABIOS*

My Voice

I was born one summer night
between two pauses. Speak to me: I'm listening.
I was born. If you could only see what suffering
the moon displays without trying.
I was born. Your name was happiness.
A hope under the radiant light, a bird.
Arriving, arriving. The sea was a pulse,
the hollow of a hand, a warm medallion.
So now they're all possible: the lights, the caresses, the skin, the horizon,
talking with words that mean nothing,
that roll around like ears or seashells,
like an open lobe that dawns
(listen, listen) in the trampled light.

TRANSLATED BY LEWIS HYDE

El vals

Eres hermosa como la piedra,
oh difunta;
oh viva, oh viva, eres dichosa como la nave.
Esta orquesta que agita
mis cuidados como una negligencia,
como un elegante biendecir de buen tono,
ignora el vello de los pubis,
ignora la risa que sale del esternón como una gran batuta.

Unas olas de afrecho,
un poco de serrín en los ojos,
o si acaso en las sienes,
o acaso adornando las cabelleras;
unas faldas largas hechas de colas de cocodrilos;
unas lenguas o unas sonrisas hechas con caparazones de cangrejos.
Todo lo que está suficientemente visto
no puede sorprender a nadie.

Las damas aguardan su momento sentadas sobre una lágrima,
disimulando la humedad a fuerza de abanico insistente.
Y los caballeros abandonados de sus traseros
quieren atraer todas las miradas a la fuerza hacia sus bigotes.
Pero el vals ha llegado.
Es una playa sin ondas,
es un entrechocar de conchas, de tacones, de espumas o de dentaduras
     postizas.
Es todo lo revuelto que arriba.

Pechos exuberantes en bandeja en los brazos,
dulces tartas caídas sobre los hombros llorosos,

THE WALTZ

You are beautiful as a stone,
O my dead woman!
O my living, living woman, you are happy as a ship!
This orchestra which stirs up
my worries like a thoughtlessness,
like an elegant witticism in a fashionable drawl,
knows nothing of the down on the secret mound,
knows nothing of the laugh which rises from the breastbone like an
	immense baton.

A few waves made of bran,
a bit of sawdust in the eyes,
or perhaps even on the temples
or perhaps decorating the women's hair.
Trailing skirts made of alligator tails,
some tongues or smiles made of the shells of crabs.
All those things that have been seen so often
can take no one by surprise.

The ladies wait for their moment seated upon a tear,
keeping their dampness hidden with a stubborn fan,
and the gentlemen, abandoned by their buttocks,
try to draw all looks toward their moustaches.
But the waltz is here.
It is a beach with no waves,
it is a clashing together of seashells, heels, foam and false teeth.
It is the churned up things arriving.

Exultant breasts on the serving tray of arms,
sweet cakes fallen on the weeping shoulders,

una languidez que revierte,
un beso sorprendido en el instante que se hacía "cabello de angel",
un dulce "sí" de cristal pintado de verde.

Un polvillo de azúcar sobre las frentes
da una blancura cándida a las palabras limadas,
y las manos se acortan más redondeadas que nunca,
mientras fruncen los vestidos hechos de esparto querido.

Las cabezas son nubes, la música es una larga goma,
las colas de plumo casi vuelan, y el estrépito
se ha convertido en los corazones en oleadas de sangre,
en un licor, si blanco, que sabe a memoria o a cita.

Adiós, adiós, esmeralda, amatista o misterio;
adiós, como una bola enorme ha llegado el instante,
el preciso momento de la desnudez cabeza abajo,
cuando los vellos van a pinchar los labios obscenos que saben.
Es el instante, el momento de decir la palabra que estalla,
el momento en que los vestidos se convertirán en aves,
las ventanas en gritos,
las luces en ¡socorro!
y ese beso que estaba (en el rincón) entre dos bocas
se convertirá en una espina
que dispensará la muerte diciendo:
Yo os amo.

FROM *ESPADAS COMO LABIOS*

a languorousness that comes over you again,
a kiss taken by surprise just as it turns into cotton candy,
a sweet "yes" of glass painted green.

Powdered sugar on the foreheads
gives a simple whiteness to the polished words
and the hands grow short, and rounder than ever
and wrinkle up the dresses as though they were sweet esparto grass.

The heads are clouds, the music is a long piece of rubber,
the tails made of lead almost fly, and the noise
has turned into waves of blood inside the heart,
and into a white liqueur that tastes of memories or a rendezvous.

Goodbye, goodbye, emerald, amethyst, secret,
goodbye, the instant has arrived like an enormous ball,
the precise moment of nakedness head down
when the downy hair begins to penetrate the obscene lips that know.
It is the instant, the moment of pronouncing the word that explodes,
the moment in which the dresses will turn into birds,
the windows into cries,
the lights into "help!"
and the kiss that was over there (in the corner) between two mouths
will be changed into a fishbone
that will distribute death saying:
I love you.

TRANSLATED BY ROBERT BLY

CON TODO RESPETO

Árboles, mujeres, y niños
son todo lo mismo: Fondo.
Las voces, los cariños, la nitidez, la alegría,
este saber que al fin estamos todos.
¡Sí! Los diez dedos que miro.

Ahora el Sol no es horrendo como una mejilla dispuesta:
no es un ropaje, ni una linterna sin habla.
No es tampoco la repuesta que se escucha con las rodillas,
o esa dificultad de tocar las fronteras con lo más blanco de los ojos.
Es ya el Sol la verdad, la lucidez, la constancia.
Se dialoga con la montaña,
se la cambia por el corazón:
se puede seguir marchando ligero.
El ojo del pez, si arribamos al río,
es justo la imagen de la dicha que Dios nos prepara,
el beso ardentísimo que nos quebranta los huesos.

Si. Al fin es la vida. Oh, qué hermosura de huevo
este amplio regalo que nos tiende ese Valle,
esta limitación sobre la que apoyar la cabeza
para oír la mejor música, la de los planetas distantes.
Vamos todos de prisa,
acerquémonos a la hoguera.
Vuestras manos de pétalos y las mías de cáscara,
estas deliciosas improvisaciojunes que nos mostramos,
valen para quemarlas, para manterer la confianza en el mañana,
para que la conversación pueda seguir ignorando la ropa.
Yo ignoro la ropa. ¿Y tú?
Yo vestido con trescientos vestidos o cáñamo,

With All Due Respect

Trees, women, and children
are all the same thing: Background.
Voices, affections, brightness, joy,
this knowledge that finally here we all are.
Indeed. Me and my ten fingers.

Now the Sun isn't horrendous like a cheek that's ready:
it isn't a piece of clothing or a speechless flashlight.
Nor is it the answer heard by our knees,
nor the task of touching the frontiers with the whitest part of our eyes.
The Sun has already become truth, lucidity, stability.
You converse with the mountain,
you trade the mountain for a heart:
then you can go on, weightless, going away.
The fish's eye, if we come to the river,
is precisely the image of happiness God sets up for us,
the passionate kiss that breaks our bones.

Indeed. Finally, it's life. Oh, what egglike beauty
in this ample gift the Valley spreads before us,
this limitation we can lean our heads against
so as to hear the greatest music, that of the distant planets.
Hurry, let's all
get close around the bonfire.
Your hands made of petals and mine of bark,
these delicious improvisations we show each other,
are good—for burning, for keeping faith in tomorrow,
so that our talk can go on ignoring our clothes.
I don't notice our clothes. Do you?
Dressed up in three hundred burlap suits,

envueltos en mis ropones más broncos,
conservo la dignidad de la aurora y alardeo de desnudeces.

Si me acariciáis yo creeré que está descargando una tormenta
y preguntaré si los rayos son de siete colores.
O a lo major estaré pensando en el aire
y en esa ligera brisa que riza la piel indefensa.

Con la punta del pie no me río,
más bien conservo mi dignidad,
y si me muevo por la escena lo hago como un excelente,
como la más incauta hormiguita.

Así por la mañana o por la tarde
cuando llegan las multitudes yo saludo con el gesto,
y no les muestro el talón porque eso es una grosería.
Antes bien, les sonrío, les tiendo la mano,
dejo escapar un pensamiento, una mariposa irisada,
mientras rubrico mi protesta convirtiéndome en estiércol.

FROM *ESPADAS COMO LABIOS*

wrapped in my roughest heaviest getup,
I maintain a dawnlike dignity and brag of how much I know about
    nakedness.

If you get close to me I'll think that a storm is breaking
and I'll ask if the thunderbolts have seven colors.
Or at best I'll be thinking about the air
and the light breeze rippling my defenseless skin.

I'm not laughing with the toe of my shoe;
instead, I'm preserving my dignity,
and if I move across the stage I do it like a rare coin,
like the craziest little ant.

And so in the morning or the afternoon
when the multitudes arrive I greet them with a grimace,
and I don't show my heel because that would be rude.
On the contrary, I smile, I shake hands,
I let loose a thought, an iridescent butterfly,
while I register my protest by turning into a turd.

TRANSLATED BY STEPHEN KESSLER

SIEMPRE

Estoy solo. Las ondas; playa, escúchame.
De frente los delfines o la espada.
La certeza de siempre, los no-límites.
Esta tierna cabeza no amarilla,
esta piedra de carne que solloza.
Arena, arena, tu clamor es mío.
Por mi sombra no existes como seno,
no finjas que las velas, que la brisa,
que un aquilón, un viento furibundo
va a empujar tu sonrisa hasta la espuma,
robándole a la sangre sus navíos.

Amor, amor, detén tu planta impura.

FROM ESPADAS COMO LABIOS

The Usual

I'm all alone. The waves; shoreline, listen to me.
In front of me, the dolphins or the sword.
The usual certainty, things without limits.
This tender head that's not yellow,
this sobbing stone made of flesh.
Sand, sand, your cry's the same as mine.
You don't live in my shadow like a breast,
you don't pretend that the sails, that the moving air,
that a wind from the north, an enraged wind
is going to shove your smile out to sea
and steal the great ships from the blood.

Love, love, restrain your sullied foot.

Translated by Lewis Hyde

MADRE, MADRE

La tristeza u hoyo en la tierra,
dulcemente cavado a fuerza de palabra,
a fuerza de pensar en el mar,
donda a merced de las ondas bogan lanchas ligeras.

Ligeras como pájaros núbiles,
amorosas como guarismos,
como ese afán postrero de besar a la orilla,
o estampa dolorida de uno solo, o pie errado.

La tristeza como un pozo en el agua,
pozo seco que ahonda el respiro de arena,
pozo.—Madre, ¿me escuchas?: eres un dulce espejo
donde una gaviota siente calor o pluma.

Madre, madre, te llamo;
espejo mío silente,
dulce sonrisa abierta como un vidrio cortado.
Madre, madre esta herida, esta mano tocada,
madre, en un pozo abierto en el pecho o extravío.

La tristeza no siempre acaba en una flor,
ni esta puede crecer hasta alcanzar el aire,
surtir.—Madre, ¿me escuchas? Soy yo que como alambre
tengo mi corazón amoroso aquí fuera.

FROM ESPADAS COMO LABIOS

MOTHER, MOTHER

Sadness, or a hollow in the earth,
gently dug through force of words,
through force of thoughts about the sea,
where frail rowboats float at the mercy of the waves.

Rowboats frail like the birds at mating time
like digits filled with love,
like that final longing to kiss the shore goodbye,
or the painful footprint of a hermit or a footstep gone astray.

Sadness like a well in the water,
a dry well that forces the sand's breathing deeper,
a well. "Mother, are you listening? You're the soft mirror
where a seagull can feel warmth or feather.

"Mother, mother, I'm calling you,
my own quiet mirror,
sweet opened smile like a piece of cut glass.
Mother, mother, this hurt, mother, this hand someone touched
is a well opened in the chest, or confusion."

Sadness doesn't always blossom as a flower,
nor the flower grow enough to overtake the air,
to spout. "Mother, are you listening to me? I'm the one
who wears love's heart here on the outside, like wire."

TRANSLATED BY TIMOTHY BALAND

TORO

Esa mentira o casta.
Aquí, mastines, pronto; paloma, vuela; salta, toro,
toro de luna o miel que no despega.
Aquí, pronto: escapad, escapad; solo quiero,
solo quiero los bordes de la lucha.

Oh tú, toro hermosísimo, piel sorprendida,
ciega suavidad como un mar hacia adentro,
quietud, caricia, toro, toro de cien poderes,
frente a un bosque parado de espanto al borde.

Toro o mundo que no,
que no muge. Silencio;
vastedad de esta hora. Cuerno o cielo ostentoso,
toro negro que aguanta caricia, seda, mano.

Ternura delicada sobre una piel de mar,
mar brillante y caliente, anca pujante y dulce,
abandono asombroso del bulto que deshace
sus fuerzas casi cósmicas como leche de estrellas.

Mano inmensa que cubre celeste toro en tierra.

From *Espadas como labios*

The Bull

That lie or breed.
Come here, dogs, quick; fly away, dove; jump, bull,
bull made of moon or honey that won't come unstuck.
Here, quick; escape everyone, escape; I only want,
I only want to be at the edge of the struggle.

Oh you, most beautiful bull, a surprised skin,
a blind smoothness like an ocean moving toward its center,
a calm, a stroking, a bull, bull of a hundred powers,
facing a forest, stopped at the edge with horror.

Bull or world that doesn't,
that doesn't bellow. Silence;
this hour's so huge. A horn or a sumptuous sky;
black bull that endures the stroking, the silk, the hand.

Fragile softness over a sea skin,
hot and lustrous sea, sweet and powerful rump,
such wonderful abandon, the way this big thing lets
its almost cosmic powers flow down like the stars' milk.

Huge hand that covers up the sky-bull on earth.

Translated by Lewis Hyde

En el fondo del pozo

(El enterrado)

Allá en el fondo del pozo donde las florecillas,
donde las lindas margaritas no vacilan,
donde no hay viento o perfume de hombre,
donde jamás el mar impone su amenaza,
allí, allí está quedo ese silencio
hecho como un rumor ahogado con un puño.

Si una abeja, si un ave voladora,
si ese error que no se espera nunca
se produce,
el frío permanence;
el sueño en vertical hundió la tierra
y ya el aire está libre.

Acaso una voz, una mano ya suelta,
un impulso hacia arriba aspira a luna,
a calma, a tibieza, a ese veneno
de una almohada en la boca que se ahoga.

¡Pero dormir es tan sereno siempre!
Sobre el frío, sobre el hielo, sobre una sombra de mejilla,
sobre una palabra yerta y, más, ya ida,
sobre la misma tierra siempre virgen.

Una tabla en el fondo, oh pozo innúmero,
esa lisura ilustre que comprueba
que una espalda es contacto, es frío seco,
es sueño siempre aunque la frente esté cerrada.

At the Bottom of the Well

(The Buried Man)

There at the bottom of the well where the little flowers,
where the pretty daisies do not wave,
where there is no wind or scent of man,
where the sea never threatens,
there, there is that still silence
like a murmur muffled with a fist.

If a bee, if a flying bird,
if that mistake which is never expected
appears,
then the cold lasts;
the dream sank the earth straight down
and now the air is free.

Perhaps a voice, a hand now free,
an upward impulse wants to be moon,
or calm, or warmth, or that poison
of a pillow in the muffled mouth.

But sleeping is always so serene!
On the cold, on the ice, on a cheek's shadow,
on a lifeless word, already gone,
on the very earth, always virgin.

A board at the bottom, oh unnumbered well,
that illustrious smoothness which proves
that a shoulder is contact, is dry cold,
is dream always though the forehead be closed.

Pueden pasar ya nubes. Nadie sabe.
Ese clamor...¿Existen las campanas?
Recuerdo que el color blanco o las formas,
recuerdo que los labios, sí, hasta hablaban.

Era el tiempo caliente.—Luz, inmólame—.
Era entonces cuando el relámpago de pronto
quedaba suspendido hecho de hierro.
Tiempo de los suspiros o de adórame,
cuando nunca las aves perdían plumas.

Tiempo de suavidad y permanencia;
los galopes no daban en el pecho,
no quedaban los cascos, no eran cera.
Las lágrimas rodaban como besos.
Y en el oído el eco era ya sólido.

Así la eternidad era el minuto.
El tiempo sólo una tremenda mano
sobre el cabello largo detenida.

O sí, en este hondo silencio o humedades,
bajo las siete capas de cielo azul yo ignoro
la música cuajada en hielo súbito,
la garganta que se derrumba sobre los ojos,
la íntima onda que se anega sobre los labios.

Dormido como una tela
siento crecer la hierba, el verde suave
que inútilmente aguarda ser curvado.

Una mano de acero sobre el césped,
un corazón, un juguete olvidado,
un resorte, una lima, un beso, un vidrio.

Clouds can now pass. No one knows.
That ringing…Do bells exist?
I remember that the color white or the forms,
I remember that the lips, yes, even spoke.

The weather was hot. —Light, consume me—.
It was then when the lightning bolt suddenly
would freeze in iron.
Time of sighs or of adore me,
when never the birds lost feathers.

Time of softness and permanence;
hoofbeats didn't pound in my chest,
the hooves didn't stay behind, they weren't wax.
Tears fell like kisses.
And in the ear the echo was already solid.

And so eternity was the minute.
Time only a huge hand
pausing over long hair.

Yes, in this deep silence or dampness,
beneath the seven layers of the blue sky I am blind to
the music jelled in sudden ice,
the throat that collapses on the eyes,
the intimate wave that is drowned on the lips.

Asleep like a cloth
I feel the grass grow, the soft green
that waits in vain to be curved.

A hand of steel on the grass,
a heart, a forgotten toy,
a coil, a file, a kiss, a piece of glass.

Una flor de metal que así impasible
chupa de tierra un silencio o memoria.

FROM *ESPADAS COMO LABIOS*

A metal flower that feels nothing
and sucks silence or memory from the earth.

Translated by Deborah Weinberger

POEMA DE AMOR

Te amo, sueño del viento;
confluyes con mis dedos olvidado del norte
en las dulces mañanas del mundo cabeza abajo
cuando es fácil sonreír porque la lluvia es blanda.

En el seno de un río viajar es delicia;
oh peces amigos, decidme el secreto de los ojos abiertos,
de las miradas mías que van a dar en la mar,
sosteniendo las quillas de los barcos lejanos.

Yo os amo, viajadores del mundo, los que dormís sobre el agua,
hombres que van a América en busca de sus vestidos,
los que dejan en la playa su desnudez dolida
y sobre las cubiertas del barco atraen el rayo de la luna.

Caminar esperando es risueño, es hermoso,
la plata y el oro no han cambiado de fondo,
botan sobre las ondas, sobre el lomo escamado
y hacen música o sueño para los pelos más rubios.

Por el fondo de un río mi deseo se marcha
de los pueblos innúmeros que he tenido en las yemas,
esas oscuridades que vestido de negro
he dejado ya lejos dibujadas en espalda.

La esperanza es la tierra, es la mejilla,
en un inmenso párpado donde yo sé que existo.
¿Te acuerdas? Para el mundo he nacido una noche
en que era suma y resta la clave de los sueños.

Peces, árboles, piedras, corazones, medallas,
sobre vuestras concéntricas ondas, sí, detenidas,

Love Poem

I love you, dream of the wind.
You merge with my fingers, are forgotten by the north
on delicate mornings of the world upside down
when it is easy to smile because the rain is soft.

It is delicious to ride in the heart of the river.
O fish friends, tell me the secret of your open eyes,
of my gazing that will flow into the sea,
holding up the keels of distant ships.

I love you, world voyagers, you who sleep on the water,
men who go to the Americas after clothing,
those who leave their aching nakedness on the beach
and draw a moonray across the shipdecks.

To journey hoping is a smile, is beautiful,
silver and gold have not changed their depths,
they toss over the waves, over the fishfins,
creating music or dream for the blondest hair.

Along the river bottom my desire departs
from innumerable villages that I held on my fingertips,
those darknesses—I was dressed in black—that I left
far away, etched on shoulders.

Hope is the earth, a cheek,
an immense eyelid where I know I exist.
Do you remember? In this world I was born one night
when adding and subtracting were the key to dreams.

Fish, trees, stones, hearts, medals,
over your concentric waves, yes, halted,

yo me muevo y, si giro, me busco, oh centro, oh centro,
camino, viajadores del mundo, del futuro existente
más allá de los mares, en mis pulsos que laten.

From Espadas como labios

I move and, circling, seek myself, O center, O center,
road, voyagers of the world, of the future existing
beyond the seas, in my pulse-beat.

Translated by Willis Barnstone

La selva y el mar

Allá por las remotas
luces o aceros aún no usados,
tigres del tamaño del odio,
leones como un corazón hirsuto,
sangre como la tristeza aplacada,
se baten como la hiena amarilla que toma la forma del poniente
    insaciable.

Oh la blancura súbita,
las ojeras violáceas de unos ojos marchitos,
cuando las fieras muestran sus espadas o dientes
como latidos de un corazón que casi todo lo ignora,
menos el amor,
al descubierto en los cuellos allá donde la arteria golpea,
donde no se sabe si es el amor o el odio
lo que reluce en los blancos colmillos.

Acariciar la fosca melena
mientras se siente la ponderosa garra en la tierra,
mientras las raíces de los árboles, temblorosas,
sienten las uñas profundas
como un amor que así invade.

Mirar esos ojos que sólo de noche fulgen,
donde todavía un cervatillo ya devorado
luce su diminuta imagen de oro nocturno,
un adiós que centellea de póstuma ternura.

El tigre, el león cazador, el elefante que en sus colmillos lleva algún
    suave collar,
la cobra que se parece al amor más ardiente,

The Jungle and the Sea

Over in the distance
near the lights or the knives that are still new,
there are tigers as big as hate
and lions like a heart covered with hair
and blood like weary sadness
and all of them are fighting with the yellow hyena who disguises him-
    self as the greedy, greedy sunset.

Such sudden whiteness
and the dark circles around those withered eyes,
when the wild animals draw their swords or teeth
like the blood out of a heart that doesn't know anything
except love,
blood that beats so clearly in those jugular veins,
and you can't tell if the thing that gleams
on their white teeth is love or hate.

To run a hand through that surly mane
while the powerful claw sticks in the ground,
while the trembling roots of trees
feel the claws go deeper
like a love that sinks in the same way.

To stare into those eyes that only burn at night,
where a little fawn, eaten a while ago, can still be seen
glowing—a tiny reflection of the black gold,
a goodbye that shines for a tenderness beyond death.

The tiger, the hunting lion, the elephant that wears some soft necklace
    around its tusks,
the cobra that looks like a lover's fire,

el águila que acaricia a la roca como los sesos duros,
el pequeño escorpión que con sus pinzas sólo aspira a oprimir un
    instante la vida,
la menguada presencia de un cuerpo de hombre que jamás podrá ser
    confundido con una selva,
ese piso feliz por el que viborillas perspicaces hacen su nido en la axila
    del musgo,
mientras la pulcra coccinela
se evade de una magnolia sedosa…
Todo suena cuando el rumor del bosque siempre virgen
    se levanta como dos alas de oro,
élitros, bronce o caracol rotundo,
frente a un mar que jamás confundirá sus espumas con las ramillas
    tiernas.

La espera sosegada,
esa esperanza siempre verde,
pájaro, paraíso, fasto de plumas no tocadas,
inventa los ramajes más altos,
donde los colmillos de música,
donde las garras poderosas, el amor que se clava,
la sangre ardiente que brota de la herida,
no alcanzará, por más que el surtidor se prolongue,
por más que los pechos entreabiertos en tierra
proyecten su dolor o su avidez a los cielos azules.

Pájaro de la dicha,
azul pájaro o pluma,
sobre un sordo rumor de fieras solitarias,
del amor o castigo contra los troncos estériles,
frente al mar remotísimo que como la luz se retira.

FROM *LA DESTRUCCIÓN O EL AMOR*

the eagle that fondles its rock as if it were a hard brain,
the little scorpion who dreams of oppressing an instant of life with
     nothing but its claws,
the foolish presence of a human body that could never be confused
     with the jungle,
and that happy level where the wise little vipers nest in the armpit of
     the moss,
while the elegant mealy bug
sneaks down a magnolia leaf that feels like silk...
And when the murmur of the forever virgin forest rises up like two
     golden wings—
wing covers, a trumpet or a rounded sounding-shell—
then the whole jungle shakes with music
in front of a sea which will never mix its waves with the small, soft
     branches.

The branches at the top
are formed by quiet waiting,
by that hope which stays green forever,
bird, paradise, elegance of untouched feathers.
The jaws of music,
the powerful claws, the love that digs itself in,
the burning blood that spatters out of a wound,
will never reach those branches. No matter how far up it spurts,
no matter how much this earth's hearts try to open
and throw their pain or their greed up into the blue sky.

Bird of happiness,
blue bird or feather,
above the deafening sound of the savage, lonesome animals,
the sound of lovemaking or the whipping of sterile tree trunks,
looking out toward the distant sea that recedes like the light.

Translated by Lewis Hyde

Unidad en ella

Cuerpo feliz que fluye entre mis manos,
rostro amado donde contemplo el mundo,
donde graciosos pájaros se copian fugitivos,
volando a la región donde nada se olvida.

Tu forma externa, diamante o rubí duro,
brillo de un sol que entre mis manos deslumbra,
cráter que me convoca con su música íntima,
con esa indescifrable llamada de tus dientes.

Muero porque me arrojo, porque quiero morir,
porque quiero vivir en el fuego, porque quiero morir,
no es mío, sino el caliente aliento
que si me acerco quema y dora mis labios desde un fondo.

Deja, deja que mire, teñido del amor,
enrojecido el rostro por tu purpúrea vida,
deja que mire el hondo clamor de tus entrañas
donde muero y renuncio a vivir para siempre.

Quiero amor o la muerte, quiero morir del todo,
quiero ser tú, tu sangre, esa lava rugiente
que regando encerrada bellos miembros extremos
siente así los hermosos límites de la vida.

Este beso en tus labios como una lenta espina,
como un mar que voló hecho un espejo,
como el brillo de un ala,
es todavía unas manos, un repasar de tu crujiente pelo,
un crepitar de la luz vengadora,

WHOLENESS WITHIN HER

Joyous flesh that flows between my hands,
lover's face where I can look upon the world,
where delicate birds copy themselves and disappear,
flying off to where nothing is forgotten.

The surface of your body, diamond or hard ruby,
sunlight that shines from between my hands,
volcano's mouth that gathers me in with its intimate music,
and your teeth calling a call no one understands.

I throw myself in and die, because I want to die,
because I want to live in fire, because this air outside
is not mine, it's the hot breath from below
that turns my lips gold and fiery when I come close.

Let me, let me, let me look—stained with love,
my face flushed red by your purple life—
let me watch the low cries in your belly
where I'm dying and throwing off this life, forever.

I want love or death, I want to be totally dead,
I want to turn into you, your blood, that roaring, confined lava
that sends our fingertips flying out, like water,
so it can feel the beautiful edges of life.

This kiss on your lips like a sleepy thorn,
like an ocean that flew up, made into a mirror,
like the shine on a wing,
this kiss is still a pair of hands, a review of your rustling hair,
a crackling noise from the grudge-bearing light,

luz o espada moral que sobre mi cuello amenaza,
pero que nunca podrá destruir la unidad de este mundo.

FROM *LA DESTRUCCIÓN O EL AMOR*

light or fatal sword that threatens my neck,

though it could never break up the wholeness of this world.

Translated by Lewis Hyde

Sin luz

El pez espada, cuyo cansancio se atribuye ante todo a la imposibilidad
de horadar a la sombra,
de sentir en su carne la frialdad del fondo de los mares donde el negror
no ama,
donde faltan aquellas frescas algas amarillas
que el sol dora en las primeras aguas.

La tristeza gemebunda de ese inmóvil pez espada cuyo ojo no gira,
cuya fijeza quieta lastima su pupila,
cuya lágrima resbala entre las aguas mismas
sin que en ellas se note su amarillo tristísimo.

El fondo de ese mar donde el inmóvil pez respira con sus branquias
un barro,
ese agua como un aire,
ese polvillo fino
que se alborota mintiendo la fantasía de un sueño,
que se aplaca monótono cubriendo el lecho quieto
donde gravita el monte altísimo, cuyas crestas se agitan
como penacho—si—de un sueño oscuro.

Arriba las espumas, cabelleras difusas,
ignoran los profundos pies de fango,
esa imposibilidad de desarraigarse del abismo,
de alzarse con unas alas verdes sobre lo seco abisal
y escaparse ligero sin miedo al sol ardiente.

Las blancas cabelleras, las juveniles dichas,
pugnan hirvientes, pobladas por los peces
—por la creciente vida que ahora empieza—,
por elevar su voz al aire joven,

LIGHTLESS

The swordfish, whose weariness arises first of all from its inability to
    pierce the shadow,
to feel in its flesh the cold unloving blackness of the sea bottom,
where there are no fresh gold seaweeds
illuminated by the sun in the first waters.

The moaning sadness of this motionless swordfish whose eye doesn't
    revolve,
whose unmoving stillness hurts its pupil,
whose tear slides through the water
without its yellow sorrow being seen.

The bottom of that ocean where the still fish breathes mud through
    its gills,
that water like an air,
that fine dust,
disturbed, which assumes the form of a dream-fantasy,
monotonously calm as it covers the still bed
where the highest mountain rests its weight, whose summits flutter
like the plumes of the same dark dream.

Above, the foam, diffuse long hair,
ignores the feet set deep in the ooze,
the impossibility of tearing free from the depth,
of rising with green wings over the abysmal drought
and flying off lightly, fearless, to the hot sun.

The long white hair, the youthful happiness,
struggles and boils, peopled with fish
—with the growing life just now beginning—
raising its voice in the young air,

donde un sol fulgurante
hace plata el amor y oro los abrazos,
las pieles conjugadas,
ese unirse los pechos como las fortalezas que se aplacan fundiéndose.

Pero el fondo palpita como un solo pez abandonado.
De nada sirve que una frente gozosa
se incruste en el azul como un sol que se da,
como amor que visita a humanas criaturas.

De nada sirve que un mar inmenso entero
sienta sus peces entre espumas como si fueran pájaros.

El calor que le roba el quieto fondo opaco,
la base inconmovible de la milenaria columna
que aplasta un ala de ruiseñor ahogado,
un pico que cantaba la evasión del amor,
gozoso entre unas plumas templadas a un sol nuevo.

Ese profundo oscuro donde no existe el llanto,
donde un ojo no gira en su cuévano seco,
pez espada que no puede horadar a la sombra,
donde aplacado el limo no imita un sueño agotado.

FROM LA DESTRUCCIÓN O EL AMOR

where the flashing sunlight
turns love silver and embraces, gold,
the conjugated skin,
that union of chests like forces calmed in fusion.

But the depth still pulses like a lone abandoned fish.
It's no use for a smiling face
to be inlaid in the blue like a given sun,
like love that visits human creatures.

It's no use for a whole huge ocean
to feel its fish dart in the foam like birds.

The heat that's stolen by the still dark depth,
the immovable base of the ancient column
that crushes the wing of a drowned nightingale,
a beak that sang of love's elusiveness,
joyous among feathers tuned to a new sun.

That profound darkness where weeping doesn't exist,
where an eye doesn't roll in its dry basket,
swordfish that can't pierce the shadow,
where calm slime doesn't imitate exhausted dreams.

TRANSLATED BY STEPHEN KESSLER

Ven siempre, ven

No te acerques. Tu frente, tu ardiente frente, tu encendida frente,
las huellas de unos besos,
ese resplandor que aun de día se siente si te acercas,
ese resplandor contagioso que me queda en las manos,
ese río luminoso en que hundo mis brazos,
en el que casi no me atrevo a beber, por temor después a ya una dura
     vida de lucero.

No quiero que vivas en mí como vive la luz,
con ese ya aislamiento de estrella que se une con su luz,
a quien el amor se niega a través del espacio
duro y azul que separa y no une,
donde cada lucero inaccesible
es una soledad que, gemebunda, envía su tristeza.

La soledad destella en el mundo sin amor.
La vida es una vívida corteza.
una rugosa piel inmóvil
donde el hombre no puede encontrar su descanso,
por más que aplique su sueño contra un astro apagado.

Pero tú no te acerques. Tu frente destellante, carbón encendido que me
     arrebata a la propia conciencia,
duelo fulgúreo en que de pronto siento la tentación de morir,
de quemarme los labios con tu roce indeleble,
de sentir mi carne deshacerse contra tu diamante abrasador.

No te acerques, porque tu beso se prolonga como el choque imposible
     de las estrellas,
como el espacio que súbitamente se incendia,

Come Always, Come

Don't come closer. Your face, your burning face, your ignited face,
the tracks of kisses,
that radiance I feel, even by daylight, when you approach,
that contagious radiance that stays on my hands,
that luminous river where I sink my arms,
from which I almost don't dare drink, for fear of a hard life of bril-
    liance later.

I don't want you to live in me like light,
with the loneliness of a star already made one with its light,
whom love denies across the hard blue space
which separates and never joins,
where each unreachable brilliance
is a solitude that moans, beaming its sadness.

Solitude flashes in the loveless world.
Life is a bright crust,
a rugged fixed skin
where man can find no rest,
however much he applies his sleep to a darkened star.

But don't come any closer. Your glowing face, live coal that stirs my
    consciousness,
the shining pain where all of a sudden I'm tempted to die,
to burn my lips on your indelible friction,
to feel my flesh melting, embraced in your burning diamond.

Don't come closer, because your kiss goes on and on like the impossi-
    ble collision of the stars,
like space that suddenly catches fire,

éter propagador donde la destrucción de los mundos
es un único corazón que totalmente se abrasa.

Ven, ven, ven como el carbón extinto oscuro que encierra una muerte;
ven como la noche ciega que me acerca su rostro;
ven como los dos labios marcados por el rojo,
por esa línea larga que funde los metales.

Ven, ven, amor mío; ven, hermética frente, redondez casi rodante
que luces como una órbita que va a morir en mis brazos;
ven como dos ojos o dos profundas soledades,
dos imperiosas llamadas de una hondura que no conozco.

¡Ven, ven, muerte, amor; ven pronto, te destruyo;
ven, que quiero matar o amar o morir o darte todo;
ven, que ruedas como liviana piedra,
confundida como una luna que me pide mis rayos!

FROM *La destrucción o el amor*

fertile ether where the destruction of worlds
is a single heart that burns itself out with love.

Come, come, come like the cold dark coal that holds a death;
come like the blind night moving its face toward me;
come like two lips branded red
on that long line that fuses metals.

Come, come, my love; come, hermetic face, roundness almost rolling,
shining like an orbit that will die in my arms;
come like two eyes or two profound solitudes,
two urgent calls from a depth I don't yet know.

Come, come, death, love; come quickly, I'll destroy you;
come, I want to kill or love or die or give you everything;
come, come rolling like a weightless stone,
confused like a moon that begs me for my light!

TRANSLATED BY STEPHEN KESSLER

VIDA

Un pájaro de papel en el pecho
dice que el tiempo de los besos no ha llegado;
vivir, vivir, el sol cruje invisible,
besos o pájaros, tarde o pronto o nunca.
Para morir basta un ruidillo,
el de otro corazón al callarse,
o ese regazo ajeno que en la tierra
es un navío dorado para los pelos rubios.
Cabeza dolorida, sienes de oro, sol que va a ponerse;
aquí en la sombra sueño con un río,
juncos de verde sangre que ahora nace,
sueño apoyado en ti calor o vida.

FROM *La destrucción o el amor*

LIFE

A paper bird I have in my chest
tells me the time for kisses has not yet come.
To live! To live!... No one sees the sun crackle,
kisses or birds, late or on time or never.
A tiny noise is enough to kill you,
the noise of some other heart falling silent,
or that far-off lap which on this earth
is a gold ship where the blond hair sails!
Head full of pain, gold temples, sun dying,
I keep dreaming of a river in this darkness,
reeds full of green blood just being born,
and I dream leaning on you, warmth or life.

TRANSLATED BY ROBERT BLY

CANCIÓN A UNA MUCHACHA MUERTA

Dime, dime el secreto de tu corazón virgen,
dime el secreto de tu cuerpo bajo tierra,
quiero saber por qué ahora eres un agua,
esas orillas frescas donde unos pies desnudos se bañan con espuma.

Dime por qué sobre tu pelo suelto,
sobre tu dulce hierba acariciada,
cae, resbala, acaricia, se va
un sol ardiente o reposado que te toca
como un viento que lleva sólo un pájaro o mano.

Dime por qué tu corazón como una selva diminuta
espera bajo tierra los imposibles pájaros,
esa canción total que por encima de los ojos
hacen los sueños cuando pasan sin ruido.

Oh tú, canción que a un cuerpo muerto o vivo,
que a un ser hermoso que bajo el suelo duerme,
cantas color de piedra, color de beso o labio,
cantas como si el nácar durmiera o respirara.

Esa cintura, ese débil volumen de un pecho triste,
ese rizo voluble que ignora el viento,
esos ojos por donde sólo boga el silencio,
esos dientes que son de marfil resguardado,
ese aire que no mueve unas hojas no verdes...

¡Oh tú, cielo riente que pasas como nube;
oh pájaro feliz que sobre un hombro ríes;
fuente que, chorro fresco, te enredas con la luna;
césped blando que pisan unos pies adorados!

FROM *La destrucción o el amor*

SONG TO A DEAD GIRL

Tell me, tell me the secret of your virgin heart,
tell me the secret your body is keeping under the ground.
I want to know why you've turned into water now,
those cool beaches where bare feet wash with surf.

Tell me why a sun falls and glides
over your loosened hair, over your sweet
smoothed grass. Why does it
caress you and leave, that burning or resting sun,
touching you like a wind that carries just a bird or a hand?

Tell me why your heart waits, like a tiny
underground forest, for the birds that won't come,
for that song our dreams will finish singing
as they pass noiselessly over our eyes.

O you, song that sings for a body, alive or dead,
for a beautiful person who sleeps under the ground,
you sing the color of stone, color of kiss or lip,
sing as if the seashell's lustre were breathing or asleep.

That belly, the frail curve of a sad breast,
your twining hair that can't feel the wind,
those eyes where nothing but silence sets sail,
those teeth of sheltered ivory,
the air that doesn't shake any ungreen leaves...

You, laughing sky that sails like a cloud!
Joyful bird that laughs on a shoulder!
Fountain, clear spring that entangles with the moon!
Soft grass, where someone's feet walk with love!

TRANSLATED BY LEWIS HYDE

SOY EL DESTINO

Sí, te he querido como nunca.

¿Por qué besar tus labios, si se sabe que la muerte está próxima,
si se sabe que amar es sólo olvidar la vida,
cerrar los ojos a lo oscuro presente
para abrirlos a los radiantes límites de un cuerpo?

Yo no quiero leer en los libros una verdad que poco a poco sube como
        un agua,
renuncio a ese espejo que dondequiera las montañas ofrecen,
pelada roca donde se refleja mi frente
cruzada por unos pájaros cuyo sentido ignoro.

No quiero asomarme a los ríos donde los peces colorados con el rubor
        de vivir,
embisten a las orillas límites de su anhelo,
ríos de los que unas voces inefables se alzan,
signos que no comprendo echado entre los juncos.

No quiero, no; renuncio a tragar ese polvo, esa tierra dolorosa, esa
        arena mordida,
esa seguridad de vivir con que la carne comulga
cuando comprende que el mundo y este cuerpo
ruedan como ese signo que el celeste ojo no entiende.

No quiero, no, clamar, alzar la lengua,
proyectarla como esa piedra que se estrella en la altura,
que quiebra los cristales de esos inmensos cielos
tras los que nadie escucha el rumor de la vida.

I Am Destiny

Yes, I've wanted you as never before.

Why kiss your lips, knowing death is near,
knowing that loving is only forgetting life,
closing our eyes against the present darkness
to open them on the shining limits of a body?

I don't want to read a truth in books that rises a little at a time like
    water,
I reject that mirror the mountains offer everywhere I look,
bald rock where my forehead is reflected
crossed by birds whose meaning escapes me.

I don't want to look into rivers where fishes ruddy with the flush
    of living
attack the banks that limit their desire,
rivers where certain unspeakable voices are lifted,
signs I fail to understand, thrown here among the rushes.

No, I don't; I refuse to swallow that dust, that aching earth, that bitten
    sand,
that certainty of living which my flesh accepts
when it learns that the world and this body
turn like a sign the celestial eye can't read.

I don't want, no, to whine and lift my tongue,
to sling it like a stone that shatters a face,
that smashes the glass of those vast skies
beyond which no one hears the sounds of life.

Quiero vivir, vivir como la hierba dura,
como el cierzo o la nieve, como el carbón vigilante,
como el futuro de un niño que todavía no nace,
como el contacto de los amantes cuando la luna los ignora.

Soy la música que bajo tantos cabellos
hace el mundo en su vuelo misterioso,
pájaro de inocencia que con sangre en las alas
va a morir en un pecho oprimido.

Soy el destino que convoca a todas los que aman,
mar único al que vendrán todos los radios amantes
que buscan a su centro, rizados por el círculo
que gira como la rosa rumorosa y total.

Soy el caballo que enciende su crin contra el pelado viento,
soy el león torturado por su propia melena,
la gacela que teme al rio indiferente,
el avasallador tigre que despuebla la selva,
el diminuto escarabajo que también brilla en el día.

Nadie puede ignorar la presencia del que vive,
del que en pie en medio de las flechas gritadas,
muestra su pecho transparente que no impide mirar,
que nunca será cristal a pesar de su claridad,
porque si acercáis vuestras manos, podréis sentir la sangre.

FROM *La destrucción o el amor*

I want to live, to live like the strong grass,
like the north wind or the snow, like the vigilant coal,
like the future of a child yet to be born,
like the contact of lovers when the moon ignores them.

I am the music the world makes in its mysterious flight
underneath all those heads of long hair,
the innocent bird with blood on its wings
that's going to die in a burdened heart.

I am the destiny summoning those who love,
the only sea where all the loving spokes
will come in search of their center, flowing on the ripples
that circulate like rumors of the absolute rose.

I am the horse that sets fire to its hair in the bald wind,
I am the lion tormented by its own mane,
the gazelle afraid of the indifferent river,
the slave-driving tiger that plunders the jungle,
the tiny beetle that also shines by daylight.

No one can ignore the presence of him who lives,
who walks upright in the crossfire
exposing his naked chest which is transparent,
which never will be glass despite its clarity,
because if your hands come near it you can feel the blood.

Translated by Stephen Kessler

Las Águilas

El mundo encierra la verdad de la vida,
aunque la sangre mienta melancólicamente
cuando como mar sereno en la tarde
siente arriba el batir de las águilas libres.

Las plumas de metal,
las garras poderosas,
ese afán del amor o la muerte,
ese deseo de beber en los ojos con un pico de hierro,
de poder al fin besar lo exterior de la tierra,
vuela como el deseo,
como las nubes que a nada se oponen,
como el azul radiante, corazón ya de afuera
en que la libertad se ha abierto para el mundo.

Las águilas serenas
no serán nunca esquifes,
no serán sueño o pájaro,
no serán caja donde olvidar lo triste,
donde tener guardado esmeraldas u ópalos.

El sol que cuaja en las pupilas,
que a las pupilas mira libremente,
es ave inmarcesible, vencedor de los pechos
donde hundir su furor contra un cuerpo amarrado.

Las violentas alas
que azotan rostros como eclipses,
que parten venas de zafiro muerto,
que seccionan la sangre coagulada,
rompen el viento en mil pedazos,

The Eagles

The earth locks up the truth about life
even though the blood tells moody lies
when, like the smooth afternoon sea,
it feels the eagles flapping freely overhead.

Their metal feathers,
their crushing claws,
that taste they have for love or death—
a longing to drink from the eyes with an iron beak,
to kiss the outside of this world once and for all—
it flies up like desire,
like the clouds that never block the way,
like the glowing blue, a heart already out there,
opening for all the world in its freedom.

The serene eagles
will never be boats,
they won't be dream or bird,
they won't be a box where sad memories lie forgotten,
where opals or emeralds are put away.

The sun that thickens in our eyes,
that gazes freely down at our eyes,
the sun is an undying bird, bully of hearts,
sinking its rage into them against a trapped body.

The violent wings
that beat faces as if they were eclipses,
that split open veins of dead sapphire,
that section up the clotted blood,
these wings break the wind into a thousand pieces—

mármol o espacio impenetrable
donde una mano muerta detenida
es el claror que en la noche fulgura.

Águilas como abismos,
como montes altísimos,
derriban majestades, troncos polvorientos,
esa verde hiedra que en los muslos
finge la lengua vegetal casi viva.

Se aproxima el momento en que la dicha consista
en desvestir de piel a los cuerpos humanos,
en que el celeste ojo victorioso
vea sólo a la tierra como sangre que gira.

Águilas de metal sonorísimo,
arpas furiosas con su voz casi humana,
cantan la ira de amar los corazones,
amarlos con las garras estrujando su muerte.

FROM *LA DESTRUCCIÓN O EL AMOR*

marble or impervious space—
where the clarity that flashes at night
is a dead hand, held back.

Eagles like deep valleys,
like high, high mountains,
they overthrow all royal things, dusty tree trunks,
the green ivy along our thighs
that pretends it's a vegetable tongue, almost alive.

The moment's coming when happiness will be a matter
of stripping the skin from human bodies,
when the gloating eye of the sky
will see the earth as nothing but blood turning in gyres.

Eagles of metal so incredibly resonant,
enraged harps with voices almost human
who sing the anger of being in love with hearts,
loving them, squeezing death out of them with their claws.

TRANSLATED BY LEWIS HYDE

No existe el hombre

Sólo la luna sospecha la verdad.
Y es que el hombre no existe.

La luna tantea por los llanos, atraviesa los ríos,
penetra por los bosques.
Modela las aún tibias montañas.
Encuentra el calor de las ciudades erguidas.
Fragua una sombra, mata una oscura esquina,
inunda de fulgurantes rosas
el misterio de las cuevas donde no huele a nada.

La luna pasa, sabe, canta, avanza y avanza sin descanso.
Un mar no es un lecho donde el cuerpo de un hombre puede tenderse
        a solas.
Un mar no es un sudario para una muerte lúcida.
La luna sigue, cala, ahonda, raya las profundas arenas.
Mueve fantática los verdes rumores aplacados.
Un cadáver en pie un instante se mece,
duda, ya avanza, verde queda inmóvil.
La luna miente sus brazos rotos,
su imponente mirada donde unos peces anidan.
Enciende las ciudades hundidas donde todavía se pueden oír
(qué dulces) las campanas vívidas;
donde las ondas posteras aún repercuten sobre los pechos neutros,
sobre los pechos blandos que algún pulpo ha adorado.

Pero la luna es pura y seca siempre.
Sale de un mar que es una caja siempre,
que es un bloque con límites que nadie, nadie estrecha,
que no es una piedra sobre un monte irradiando.

MAN DOESN'T EXIST

Only the moon suspects the truth.
And it's that man doesn't exist.

The moon feels its way over the fields and crosses the rivers,
it probes into the woods.
It gives a shape to the still warm mountains.
It runs into the heat from built-up cities.
It forms a shadow and kills a dark corner,
and its flashing roses flood
the mystery of the caves where there is no odor.

The moon chants a tune and understands and moves and goes on and
    on without stopping.
An ocean isn't a bed where a man's body can stretch out all alone.
An ocean isn't a shroud to cover a shining death.
The moon keeps going; it scratches and soaks and sinks into the
    packed sand.
It gives the calm green murmurs an incredible motion.
A corpse stands up and sways for a moment,
he wavers and then goes on. He stops, green and still.
The moon alters his broken arms,
his stern gaze where some fish are nestling.
The moon sets fire to the sunken cities where you can still hear
(how pleasing!) the clear bells;
where the last ripples still echo over the neuter breasts,
over the soft breasts that some octopus has worshipped.

But the moon is always pure and dry.
It comes from an ocean that's always a container,
that's a block of stone whose limits no one, no one can cut down,
an ocean that isn't a rock glowing on top of a mountain.

Sale y persigue lo que fuera los huesos,
lo que fuera las venas de un hombre,
lo que fuera su sangre sonada, su melodiosa cárcel,
su cintura visible que a la vida divide,
o su cabeza ligera sobre un aire hacia oriente.

Pero el hombre no existe.
Nunca ha existido, nunca.
Pero el hombre no vive, como no vive el día.
Pero la luna inventa sus metales furiosos.

FROM *MUNDO A SOLAS*

The moon comes out and chases what used to be a man's bones,
what used to be his blood vessels,
what used to be his sonorous blood, his prison full of songs,
his visible waist that divides life,
or his light head going east on the wind.

But man doesn't exist.
He has never existed, never.
But man doesn't live, as the day doesn't live.
But the moon invents his furious metals.

TRANSLATED BY LEWIS HYDE

El árbol

El árbol jamás duerme.
Dura pierna de roble, a veces tan desnuda quiere un sol muy oscuro.
Es un muslo piafante que un momento se para,
mientras todo el horizonte se retira con miedo.

Un árbol es un muslo que en la tierra se yergue como la erecta vida.
No quiere ser ni blanco ni rosado,
y es verde, verde siempre como los duros ojos.

Rodilla inmensa donde los besos no imitarán jamás falsas hormigas.
Donde la luna no pretenderá ser un sutil encaje.
Porque la espuma que una noche osara hasta rozarlo
a la mañana es roca, dura roca sin musgo.

Venas donde a veces los labios que las besan
sienten el brío del acero que cumple,
sienten ese calor que hace la sangre brillante
cuando escapa apretada entre los sabios músculos.

Sí. Una flor quiere a veces ser un brazo potente.
Pero nunca veréis que un árbol quiera ser otra cosa.
Un corazón de un hombre a veces resuena golpeando.
Pero un árbol es sabio, y plantado domina.

Todo un cielo o un rubor sobre sus ramas descansa.
Cestos de pájaros niños no osan colgar de sus yemas.
Y la tierra está quieta toda ante vuestros ojos;
pero yo sé que ella se alzaría como un mar por tocarle.

En lo sumo, gigante, sintiendo las estrellas todas rizadas sin un viento,
resonando misteriosamente sin ningún viento dorado,

THE TREE

The tree never sleeps.
Strong leg of oak, sometimes so naked, it wants a sun that's very dark.
It's a thigh that stamps the ground and then pauses for a moment
while the whole horizon retreats in fear.

A tree is a thigh that grows on the earth like life standing up.
It doesn't want to be white or pink
and it's green, always green like hard eyes.

Immense knee where kisses will never try to act like false ants.
Where the moon won't pretend to be a piece of fine lace.
Because the white foam that might even dare graze it one night
is stone in the morning, hard stone without moss.

Where sometimes the lips that kiss the blood vessels
can feel the shine of the weapon that does its duty,
and feel that heat given off by the brilliant blood
as it slips away, squeezed between the wise muscles.

Yes. Sometimes a flower wants to be a mighty arm.
But you'll never see a tree that wants to be anything else.
Sometimes a man's heart pounds with sound.
But a tree is wise and rules where it's rooted.

The whole sky or a blush rests on its branches.
The baskets of baby birds are afraid to hang from its buds.
And the earth is all still before our eyes.
But I know she could swell up like a sea and touch it.

At the top, gigantic, feeling all the stars curled without wind,
making a mysterious music with no golden wind,

un árbol vive y puede pero no clama nunca,
ni a los hombres mortales arroja nunca su sombra.

FROM MUNDO A SOLAS

a tree is alive and it can cry out but never does,
and it never throws its shadow down for men, who must die.

Translated by Lewis Hyde

Bajo la tierra

No. No. Nunca. Jamás.
Mi corazón no existe.
Será inútil que vosotros, uno a uno, como árboles desnudos,
paséis cuando la tierra gira.
Inútil la luz suene en las hojas como un viento querido
e imite dulcemente un corazón que llama.

No. Yo soy la sombra oscura que en las raíces de los árboles
se curva como serpiente emitiendo una música.
Serpiente gruesa que como tronco de árbol
bajo tierra respira sin sospechar un césped.

Yo sé que existe un cielo. Acaso un Dios que sueña.
Sé que ese azul radiante que lleváis en los ojos
es un cielo pequeño con un oro dormido.

Bajo tierra se vive. La humedad es la sangre.
Hay lombrices pequeñas como niños no nacidos.
Hay tubérculos que hacia dentro crecen como las flores.
Ignoran que en lo sumo y en libertad los pétalos
son rosas, amarillos, carmines o inocentes.

Hay piedras que nunca serán ojos. Hay hierbas que son saliva triste.
Hay dientes en la tierra que en medio de los sueños
se mueven y mastican lo que nunca es el beso.

Debajo de la tierra hay, más honda, la roca,
la desnuda, la purísima roca donde sólo podrían vivir seres humanos,
donde el calor es posible a las carnes desnudas
que allí aplicadas serían flores soberbias, límpidas.

Under the Ground

No. No. No more. Never.
My heart doesn't exist.
It would be useless for all of you to pass by,
one by one, like leafless trees, while the earth turns.
Useless for the light to hum in the leaves like a wind we love
and sweetly pretend to be a heart that calls out.

No, I am the dark shadow coiled among tree roots
like a serpent sending out music.
A fleshy snake who, like a tree trunk under the ground,
breathes and never suspects there's grass up above.

I know the sky exists. Maybe a God who dreams.
I know that the radiant blue you carry in your eyes
is a small sky with gold sleeping in it.

We live underground. The moisture is blood.
There are tiny earthworms like unborn children.
There are tubers that blossom inward like flowers.
They don't know that up above the petals are free to be
pinks, yellows, carmines, or harmless.

There are stones that will never be eyes; grasses that are sad saliva.
And teeth in the earth that stir during dreams
and chew something that's never a kiss.

Under the ground there is, still deeper, the rock,
the bare, most pure rock where only human beings could live,
where warmth is possible for naked bodies
which, placed there, would be proud, clear flowers.

Hay agua bajo la tierra. Agua oscura, ¿sabéis?
Agua sin cielo.
Agua que muda espera por milenios el rostro,
el puro o cristalino rostro que se refleje,
o ese plumón de pájaro que rasga un cielo abierto.

Más hondo, más, el fuego purifica.
Es el fuego desierto donde nunca descienden.
Destierro prohibido a las almas, a las sombras.
Entrañas que se abrasan de soledad sin numen.

No sois vosotros, los que vivís en el mundo,
los que pasáis o dormís entre blancas cadenas,
los que voláis acaso con nombre de poniente,
o de aurora o de cenit,
no sois los que sabréis el destino de un hombre.

FROM *MUNDO A SOLAS*

92

There is water under the ground. Dark water, see?
Water with no sky.
Water that silently waits millenniums for the face,
the pure or crystalline face that is reflected,
or the feather that rips through an open sky.

Deeper, much deeper, the fire purifies.
It is the wilderness fire to which no one descends.
An exile forbidden to souls, forbidden to shadows.
Bowels that burn with an unholy solitude.

It won't be you, all of you who live in the world,
you who walk or sleep among white chains,
you who fly perhaps with the name of the west,
or of the dawn or of glory,
it won't be you who'll come to know the fate of a man.

TRANSLATED BY LEWIS HYDE AND DAVID UNGER

El sol victorioso

No pronuncies mi nombre
imitando a los árboles que sacuden su triste cabellera,
empapada de luna en las noches de agosto
bajo un cielo morado donde nadie ha vivido.

No me llames
como llama a la tierra su viento que no la toca,
su triste viento u oro que rozándola pasa,
sopechando el carbón que vigilante encierra.

Nunca me digas que tu sombra es tan dura
como un bloque con límites que en la sombra reposa,
bloque que se dibuja contra un cielo parado,
junto a un lago sin aire, bajo una luna vacía.

El sol, el fuerte, el duro y brusco sol que deseca pantanos,
que atiranta los labios, que cruje como hojas secas entre los labios
    mismos,
que redondea rocas peladas como montes de carne,
como redonda carne que pesadamente aguanta la caricia tremenda,
la mano poderosa que estruja masas grandes,
que ciñe las caderas de esos tremendos cuerpos
que los ríos aprietan como montes tumbados.

El sol despeja siempre noches de luna larga,
interminables noches donde los filos verdes,
donde los ojos verdes,
donde las manos verdes
son sólo verdes túnicas, telas mojadas verdes,
son sólo pechos verdes,
son sólo besos verdes entre moscas ya verdes.

THE VICTORIOUS SUN

Don't speak my name, pretending
you're those trees that shake their sad, hairy heads,
drenched with moonlight on August nights
under a purple sky where no one has lived.

Don't call me
the way the wind calls to the earth without touching it,
the sad wind or gold that grazes it and goes on,
thinking of the coal that's carefully confined.

Never tell me that your shadow is as hard
as a cut slab of stone resting in the shade,
a slab that stands out against a still sky,
on the edge of a windless lake, under an empty moon.

The sun, the strong, hard and rough sun that dries up swamps,
that tightens lips, that rustles like dry leaves between those same lips,
that smooths barren rocks like heaps of flesh,
like smooth flesh which sluggishly carries the huge caress,
the powerful hand that crushes great masses,
that clasps the hips of those huge bodies
which rivers squeeze as if they were fallen forests.

The sun always clears away the long-mooned nights,
unending nights where green blades,
green eyes,
green hands,
are nothing but green robes, wet green fabrics,
nothing but green breasts,
green kisses among already green flies.

El sol o mano dura,
o mano roja, o furia, o ira naciente.
El sol hace a la tierra una escoria sin muerte.

No, no digas mi nombre como luna encerrada,
como luna que entre los barrotes de una jaula nocturna
bate como los pájaros, como quizá los ángeles,
como los verdes ángeles que en un agua han vivido.

Huye, como huiría el pantano que un hombre ha visto formarse sobre
    su pecho,
crecer sobre su pecho,
y ha visto que su sangre como nenúfar surte,
mientras su corazón bulle como oculta burbuja.

Las mojadas raíces
que un hombre siente en su pecho, bajo la noche apagada,
no son vida ni muerte, sino quietud o limo,
sino pesadas formas de culebras de agua
que entre la carne viven sin un musgo horadado.

No, no digas mi nombre,
noche horrenda de agosto, de un imposible enero;
no, no digas mi nombre,
pero mátame, oh sol, con tu justa cuchilla.

FROM MUNDO A SOLAS

The sun or the rough hand,
or red hand, or fury, or rising anger.
The sun that makes the earth a piece of slag that won't die.

No, don't say my name as if it were an imprisoned moon,
a moon that flaps about inside the bars of a night cage
like birds, maybe like angels,
like those green angels who have lived in water.

Get away, get away like the swamp that a man has seen forming on his
    chest,
swelling over his chest,
a man who's seen his blood spout like a white water lily,
while his heart boils like a hidden bubble.

The damp roots
that a man feels in his chest, beneath the extinguished night,
are neither life nor death, but peace or mud
or the heavy shapes of snakes made of water
that live in the flesh where there is no moss full of holes.

No, don't say my name,
hideous night in August or January that cannot be;
no, don't say my name,
but kill me, O sun, with your impartial blade.

Translated by Lewis Hyde and David Unger

Guitarra o luna

Guitarra como luna.
¿Es la luna o su sangre?
Es un mínimo corazón que ha escapado
y que sobre los bosques va dejando su azul música insomne.

Una voz o su sangre,
una pasión o su horror,
una pez o luna seca
que colea en la noche salpicando los valles.

Mano profunda o ira amenazada.
¿La luna es roja o amarilla?
No, no es un ojo inyectado en la furia
de presenciar los límites de la tierra pequeña.

Mano que por los cielos busca la misma vida,
busca los pulsos de un cielo desangrándose,
busca en las entrañas entre los viejos planetas
que extrañan la guitarra que se alumbra en la noche.

Pena, pena de un pecho que nadie define,
cuando las fieras sienten sus pelos erizados,
cuando se sienten empapadas en la luz fría
que les busca la piel como una mano quimérica.

FROM *MUNDO A SOLAS*

Guitar or Moon

A guitar like a moon.
Is it the moon or only its blood?
It's a tiny heart that has escaped
and goes over the woods trailing its blue, sleepless music.

A voice or its blood,
a passion or its terror,
a fish or a dry moon
that flops about at night, splashing the valleys.

Strange hand or threatening anger.
Is the moon red or yellow?
No, it's not an eye turned bloodshot in its rage
to see the edges of the tiny earth.

Hand that searches through the sky for life itself,
that searches for the heartbeat of a bleeding sky,
that searches deep in the middle of the old planets
who miss the guitar that shines in the night.

Grief, grief of a breast no one can quite describe,
when wild animals feel their hair bristling,
when they feel themselves soaked in the cold light
that hunts for their skins like a monstrous hand.

Translated by Lewis Hyde and David Unger

Destino trágico

Confundes ese mar silencioso que adoro
con la espuma instantánea del viento entre los árboles.

Pero el mar es distinto.
No es viento, no es su imagen.
No es el resplandor de un beso pasajero,
ni es siquiera el gemido de unas alas brillantes.

No confundáis sus plumas, sus alisadas plumas,
con el torso de una paloma.
No penséis en el pujante acero del águila.
Por el cielo las garras poderosas detienen el sol.
Las águilas oprimen a la noche que nace,
la estrujan—todo un río de último resplandor va a los mares—
y la arrojan remota, despedida, apagada,
allí donde el sol de mañana duerme niño sin vida.

Pero el mar, no. No es piedra,
esa esperalda que todos amasteis en las tardes sedientas.
No es piedra rutilante toda labios tendiéndose,
aunque el calor tropical haga a la playa latir,
sintiendo el rumoroso corazón que la invade.

Muchas veces pensasteis en el bosque.
Duros mástiles altos,
árboles infinitos
bajo las ondas adivinasteis poblados de unos pájaros de espumosa
    blancura.
Visteis los vientos verdes
inspirados moverlos,
y escuchasteis los trinos de unas gargantas dulces:

Tragic Destiny

You confuse the silent sea I love
with the momentary surf of the wind through the trees.

But the sea's not like that,
not the wind, nor the image of wind,
not the radiance of the passing kiss,
not even the moaning of brilliant wings.

Don't confuse its feathers, its sleek feathers,
with the breast of a dove.
Don't think of the eagle's sinewy steel.
Its powerful talons halt the sun in the sky.
The eagles oppress the night at its birth,
they crush it—a whole river of dying splendor flows to the sea—
and they throw it way out, discarded, extinguished,
to where tomorrow's sun sleeps like a lifeless child.

But no, not the sea. It isn't stone,
that emerald all of you loved on thirsty afternoons.
Nor is it a stone flashing its extended lips,
even though the tropical heat makes the beach throb,
feeling the murmuring heart that invades it.

You often thought of the forest,
hard and tall masts under the waves,
innumerable trees
you imagined alive with foamy white birds.
You saw the green winds,
inspired, move the trees
and heard the warble of sweet-sounding throats:

ruiseñor de los mares, noche tenue sin luna,
fulgor bajo las ondas donde pechos heridos
cantan tibios en ramos de coral con perfume.

Ah, sí, yo sé lo que adorasteis.
Vosotros pensativos en la orilla,
con vuestra mejilla en la mano aún mojada,
mirasteis esas ondas, mientras acaso pensabais en un cuerpo:
un solo cuerpo dulce de un animal tranquilo.
Tendisteis vuestra mano y aplicasteis su calor
a la tibia tersura de una piel aplacada.
¡Oh suave tigre a vuestros pies dormido!

Sus dientes blancos visibles en las fauces doradas,
brillaban ahora en paz. Sus ojos amarillos,
minúsculas guijas casi de nácar al poniente,
cerrados, eran todo silencio ya marino.
Y el cuerpo derramado, veteado sabiamente de una onda poderosa,
era bulto entregado, caliente, dulce solo.

Pero de pronto os levantasteis.
Habíais sentido las alas oscuras,
envío mágico del fondo que llama a los corazones.
Mirasteis fijamente el empezado rumor de los abismos.
¿Qué formas contemplasteis? ¿Qué signos, inviolados,
qué precisas palabras que la espuma decía,
dulce saliva de unos labios secretos
que se entreabren, invocan, someten, arrebatan?
El mensaje decía...

Yo os vi agitar los brazos. Un viento huracando
movió vuestros vestidos iluminados por el poniente trágico.
Vi vuestra cabellera alzarse traspasada de luces,
y desde lo alto de una roca instantánea

nightingale of the sea, dim and moonless night,
brilliance under the waves where warm, wounded breasts
sing on bouquets of perfumed coral.

Yes, I know what you loved,
brooding by the shore,
your cheek in your still-damp hand,
thinking, maybe, of a body,
the one sweet body of a quiet animal.
Spreading your hand you placed its warmth
on the calm fur's cool gloss.
Oh smooth tiger sleeping at your feet!

His white teeth visible in the golden throat
were glittering now in peace. His yellow eyes —
small round stones almost iridescent at sunset—
were closed and silent now as the sea.
And the extravagant body, striped with purpose by a powerful wave,
was a surrendered form, hot, sweet, alone.

But suddenly you got up.
You had felt the dark wings,
magic token from the depths that calls out to our hearts.
You stared at the murmur that now starts in the depths.
What shapes did you imagine? What sacred symbols,
what precise words did the surf speak,
sweet saliva from secret lips
that open slightly, naming, mesmerizing, stealing away?
The message said...

I saw you waving your arms. A wind like a hurricane
disturbed your clothes lit up by the tragic sunset.
I saw your hair rise up, shot through with lights,
and from the height of a momentary rock

presencié vuestro cuerpo hendir los aires
y caer espumante en los senos del agua;
vi dos brazos largos surtir de la negra presencia
y vi vuestra blancura, oí el último grito,
cubierto rápidamente por los trinos alegres de los ruiseñores del fondo.

FROM *SOMBRA DEL PARAÍSO*

I saw your body split the winds
and fall foaming into the breasts of water;
I saw two long arms rise from the black display
and I saw your whiteness, I heard the last cry,
covered quickly by the cheerful warble of nightingales from the deep.

TRANSLATED BY PILAR ZALAMEA AND ALLEN KIMBRELL

Destino de la carne

No, no es eso. No miro
del otro lado del horizonte un cielo.
No contemplo unos ojos tranquilos, poderosos,
que aquieten a las aguas feroces que aquí braman.
No miro esa cascada de luces que descienden
de una boca hasta un pecho, hasta unas manos blandas,
finitas, que a este mundo contienen, atesoran.

Por todas partes veo cuerpos desnudos, fieles
al cansancio del mundo. Carne fugaz que acaso
nació para ser chispa de luz, para abrasarse
de amor y ser la nada sin memoria, la hermosa
redondez de la luz.
Y que aquí está, aquí está, marchitamente eterna,
sucesiva, constante, siempre, siempre cansada.

Es inútil que un viento remoto, con forma vegetal, o una lengua,
lama despacio y largo su volumen, lo afile,
lo pula, lo acaricie, lo exalte.
Cuerpos humanos, rocas cansadas, grises bultos
que a la orilla del mar conciencia siempre
tenéis de que la vida no acaba, no, heredándose.
Cuerpos que mañana repetidos, infinitos, rodáis
como una espuma lenta, desengañada, siempre.
¡Siempre carne del hombre, sin luz! Siempre rodados
desde allá, de un océano sin origen que envía
ondas, ondas, espumas, cuerpos cansados, bordes
de un mar que no se acaba y que siempre jadea en sus orillas.

WHAT HAPPENS TO ALL FLESH

No, there's none of that. I don't see
any heaven on the far side of the horizon.
I can't see any calm, powerful eyes
to still the thrashing waters we hear howling here.
I don't see the waterfall of lights that goes
from a mouth to a breast, descending, to some bland
and bounded hands that enclose this world, hoard it.

All I can see are naked bodies, faithful
to the weariness of the world. Dying flesh, born I suppose
to be a chip of light, to burn itself up
with lovemaking and be the *nada* without memory, the beautiful
roundness of light.
And this flesh is here, it's here, eternal in a feeble way,
over and over, constant and tired forever, forever.

It's no use for a distant, plant-shaped wind, or a tongue
to lick this lump of flesh slowly all over, to wear it down,
polish it, stroke it, worship it.
Human bodies, exhausted rocks, gray sacks
on the seashore, you always understand that life
never ends—it just inherits itself.
You endlessly repeated bodies roll out every morning
like a slow and disenchanted wave.
Human flesh forever, no light! Always rolled
from over there, from a sourceless ocean that sends out
wave on wave, the swells, the tired bodies, the borders
of a sea that never quits, that gasps on its shores, forever.

Todos, multiplicados, repetidos, sucesivos, amontonáis la carne,
la vida, sin esperanza, monótonamente iguales bajo los cielos hoscos
      que impasibles se heredan.
Sobre ese mar de cuerpos que aquí vierten sin tregua, que aquí rompen
redondamente y quedan mortales en las playas,
no se ve, no, ese rápido esquife, ágil velero
que con quilla de acero, rasgue, sesgue,
abra sangre de luz y raudo escape
hacia el hondo horizonte, hacia el origen
último de la vida, al confín del océano eterno
que humanos desparrama
sus grises cuerpos. Hacia la luz, hacia esa escala ascendente de brillos
que de un pecho benigno hacia una boca sube,
hacia unos ojos grandes, totales que contemplan,
hacia unas manos mudas, finitas, que aprisionan,
donde cansados siempre, vitales, aún nacemos.

FROM SOMBRA DEL PARAÍSO

108

All of you, innumerable, cloned, over and over, heaping up your flesh,
your lives, without hope, all monotonously the same under the sullen
    skies that feel nothing and repeat.
That sea never ceases pouring out the bodies, and they break here,
roundly, and lie dying on the beaches.
And no one sees that swift ship, no one sees it, the quick sail
whose steel bow could slant and slice
and open up the luminous blood and then race off
into the deep horizon, toward the last
source of life, the boundary of the eternal sea
that pours out these gray
human corpses. Toward the light, toward that rising ladder of bright
    things
that climbs from a loving breast to a mouth, ascending,
to some huge, full eyes that watch us,
to some silent, bounded hands that make a prison
where we're still being born, charged with energy, always tired.

Translated by Lewis Hyde

LAS MANOS

Mira tu mano, que despacio se mueve,
transparente, tangible, atravesada por la luz,
hermosa, viva, casi humana en la noche.
Con reflejo de luna, con dolor de mejilla, con vaguedad de sueño
mírala así crecer, mientras alzas el brazo,
búsqueda inútil de una noche perdida,
ala de luz que cruzando en silencio
toca carnal esa bóveda oscura.

No fosforece tu pesar, no ha atrapado
ese caliente palpitar de otro vuelo.
Mano volante perseguida: pareja.
Dulces, oscuras, apagadas, cruzáis.

Sois las amantes vocaciones, los signos
que en la tiniebla sin sonido se apelan.
Cielo extinguido de luceros que, tibio,
campo a los vuelos silenciosos te brindas.

Manos de amantes que murieron, recientes,
manos con vida que volantes se buscan
y cuando chocan y se estrechan encienden
sobre los hombres una luna instantánea.

FROM *SOMBRA DEL PARAÍSO*

THE HANDS

Look at your hand, how slowly it moves,
transparent, tangible, cut through with light,
beautiful, alive, almost human in the night.
With the moon's reflection, with the pain in a cheek, with the
     vagueness of dreams
look at how it grows as you raise your arm,
fruitless search for a lost darkness,
wing of light that moves across in silence
and feels that dark crypt with its flesh.

Your sorrow doesn't phosphoresce, it hasn't caught
the other wing's hot heartbeat.
A flying hand being chased: a couple.
Sweet, dark and faded, you cross back and forth.

You are the calling of lovers, the signals
that silently appeal to one another in the dark.
Sky with rubbed-out stars, you give yourself,
like a warm field, to these noiseless wings.

Hands of lovers who have recently died,
hands full of life that fly after each other
and, when they collide and clasp, light up
a momentary moon over the world of men.

TRANSLATED BY LEWIS HYDE

EL CUERPO Y EL ALMA

Pero es más triste todavía, mucho más triste.
Triste como la rama que deja caer su fruto para nadie.
Más triste, más. Como ese vaho
que de la tierra exhala después la pulpa muerta.
Como esa mano que del cuerpo tendido
se eleva y quiere solamente acariciar las luces,
la sonrisa doliente, la noche aterciopelada y muda.
Luz de la noche sobre el cuerpo tendido sin alma.
Alma fuera, alma fuera del cuerpo, planeando
tan delicadamente sobre la triste forma abandonada.
Alma de niebla dulce, suspendida
sobre su ayer amante, cuerpo inerme
que pálido se enfría con las nocturnas horas
y queda quieto, solo, dulcemente vacío

Alma de amor que vela y se separa
vacilando, y al fin se aleja tiernamente fría.

FROM SOMBRA DEL PARAÍSO

The Body and the Soul

But it is sadder than that, much, much sadder.
Sad as a branch letting its fruit fall for no one.
Sadder, much sadder. Like the mist
the dead fruit breathes out from the ground.
Like that hand that rises from the corpse lying in state
and merely wants to touch the lamps,
the grieving smile, the night speechless and velvet.
Luminous night above the corpse stretched out without its soul.
The soul outside, soul outside the body, swooping
with such delicacy over the shape sad and abandoned.
Soul of soft mist, held floating
above its former lover, the defenseless and pale
body, which grows colder as the night goes on,
it remains silent, alone, empty in a gentle way.

Soul of love that watches and hesitates
to free itself, but finally leaves, gentle and cold.

TRANSLATED BY ROBERT BLY

LOS INMORTALES

I
La lluvia

La cintura no es rosa.
No es ave. No son plumas.
La cintura es la lluvia,
fragilidad, gemido
que a ti se entrega. Ciñe,
mortal, tú con tu brazo
un agua dulce, queja
de amor. Estrecha, estréchala.
Toda la lluvia un junco
parece. ¡Cómo ondula,
si hay viento, si hay tu brazo,
mortal que, hoy sí, la adoras!

II
El sol

Leve, ingrávida, apenas,
la sandalia. Pisadas
sin carne. Diosa sola,
demanda a un mundo planta
para su cuerpo, arriba
solar. No cabellera
digáis; cabello ardiente.
Decid sandalia, leve
pisada; decid sólo,
no tierra, grama dulce
que cruje a ese destello,
tan suave que la adora

The Immortals

I
Rain

The waist is not a rose.
Not a bird. Not feathers.
The waist is the rain,
fragility, a moan
giving itself to you. Use
your mortal arm to hug
fresh water, a love
complaint. Embrace, embrace it!
The entire rain looks like
a single reed. How it wavers
if there is a wind, if your mortal arm
is there, yes, today, you who love it!

II
Sun

Light, almost weightless:
the sandal. Footsteps
with no flesh. Solitary goddess,
from a world she demands walking space
for her body high
and solar. Don't say long
hair; burning hair.
Say sandal, light
footstep; don't say
earth, but fresh grass
crackling in that flash,
so soft that it loves her

cuando la pisa. ¡Oh, siente
tu luz, tu grave tacto
solar! Aquí, sintiéndote,
la tierra es cielo. Y brilla.

III
La palabra

La palabra fue un día
calor: un labio humano.
Era la luz como mañana joven; más: relámpago
en esta eternidad desnuda. Amaba
alguien. Sin antes ni después. Y el verbo
brotó. ¡Palabra sola y pura
por siempre—Amor—en el espacio bello!

IV
La tierra

La tierra conmovida
exhale vegetal
su gozo. ¡Hela: ha nacido!
Verde rubor, hoy boga
por un espacio aún nuevo.
¿Qué encierra? Sola, pura
de sí, nadie la habita.
Sólo la gracia muda,
primigenia, del mundo
va en astros, leve, virgen,
entre la luz dorada.

when she walks on it. Oh feel
your light, your grave solar
touch! Here, feeling you,
the earth is sky. And shines.

III
Word

One day the word was
heat: a human lip.
It was the light of young mornings; more: lightning
in this naked eternity. Someone
loved. With no before or after. And the logos
was born. Word alone and pure
forever—Love—in beautiful space!

IV
Earth

Deeply moved, the earth
exhales its vegetable
joy. Look: it is born!
Green blush, today it sails
through a still new space.
What does it enclose? Alone, pure in
itself, no one inhabits it.
Only the mute primigenial
grace of the earth
moves in stars—airy, virgin—
in the gold light.

V

El fuego

Todo el fuego suspende
la pasión . ¡Luz es sola!
Mirad cuán puro se alza
hasta lamer los cielos,
mientras las aves todas
por él vuelan. ¡No abrasa!
¿Y el hombre? Nunca. Libre
todavía de ti,
humano, está ese fuego.
Luz es, luz inocente.
¡Humano: nunca nazcas!

VI

El aire

Aún más que el mar, el aire,
más inmenso que el mar, está tranquilo.
Alto velar de lucidez sin nadie.
Acaso la corteza pudo un día,
de la tierra, sentirte, humano. Invicto,
el aire ignora que habitó en tu pecho.
Sin memoria, immortal, el aire esplende.

VII

El mar

¿Quién dijo acaso que la mar suspira,
labio de amor hacia las playas, triste?
Dejad que envuelta por la luz campee.
¡Gloria, Gloria en la altura, y en la mar, el oro!

V
Fire

The whole fire dangles
passion. Light alone!
Look how pure it ascends
till it licks the skies,
while all the birds
fly through it. It doesn't burn!
And man? Never. That fire
is still
free of you.
It is light, innocent light.
Human beings, never be born!

VI
Air

Even more than the sea, the air—
huger than the sea—is calm.
High unpeopled vigil of lucidity.
Perhaps one day the crust of earth
could feel you, human. But the unconquered
air doesn't know it lived in your chest.
No memory, deathless, the air glitters.

VII
Sea

Who said perhaps that the sea moans
sadly, lip of love, toward the beaches?
Let it spread out, enveloped in light.
Glory, glory on high, and on the sea, gold!

¡Ah soberana luz que envuelve, canta
la inmarcesible edad del mar gozante!
Allá, reverberando
sin tiempo, el mar existe.
¡Un corazón de dios sin muerte, late!

FROM *SOMBRA DEL PARAÍSO*

Ah, sovereign light that envelops, sings
the imperishable age of the sensual sea!
There, reverberating
timeless, the sea exists.
Heart of a deathless god, throbbing!

Translated by Willis Barnstone
and David Garrison

El poeta

Para ti, que conoces cómo la piedra canta,
y cuya delicada pupila sabe ya del peso una montaña sobre un ojo dulce,
y cómo el resonante clamor de los bosques se aduerme suave un día en
      nuestras venas;

para ti, poeta, que sentiste en tu aliento
la embestida brutal de las aves celestes,
y en cuyas palabras tan pronto vuelan las poderosas alas de las águilas
como se ve brillar el lomo de los calientes peces sin sonido:

oye este libro que a tus manos envío
con ademán de selva,
pero donde de repente una gota fresquísima de rocío brilla sobre una
      rosa,
o se ve batir el deseo del mundo,
la tristeza que como párpado doloroso
cierra el poniente y oculta el sol como una lágrima oscurecida,
mientras la immensa frente fatigada
siente un beso sin luz, un beso largo,
unas palabras mudas que habla el mundo finando.

Si, poeta: el amor y el dolor son tu reino.
Carne mortal la tuya, que, arrebatada por el espíritu,
arde en la noche o se eleva en el mediodía poderoso,
immensa lengua profética que lamiendo los cielos
ilumina palabras que dan muerte a los hombres.

La juventud de tu corazón no es una playa
donde la mar embiste con sus espumas rotas,
dientes de amor que mordiendo los bordes de la tierra,
braman dulce a los seres.

THE POET

This is for you who have seen how the stone sings,
who found out how heavy a mountain weighs on a delicate eye,
and how, one day, the windy cry of the forest gently falls asleep in our
    blood;

in your breath, poet, you have felt
the animal attack of the birds of heaven,
and powerful eagle wings flash in your words
the way the bellies of hot fish gleam without a sound:

listen to this book I put in your hands
with my forest gestures,
but where an incredibly fresh dewdrop suddenly shines on a rose,
or where the lust of the world can be seen thrashing about,
the sadness (like a melancholy eyelid)
that closes the dusk and hides the sun like a clouded tear,
while the huge, exhausted forehead
feels a kiss without light, a slow kiss,
a few silent words spoken by the darkening world.

Yes, love and suffering are your kingdom.
Yours, the body that dies. Carried off by the spirit
it burns at night or rises up in the powerful daylight,
huge, prophetic tongue that licks the sky,
lighting up the words that send men to their deaths.

The youthfulness of your heart is not a shore
where the sea charges with its smashed whitecaps,
love teeth that bite at the edges of the earth
and bellow sweetly at its creatures.

No es ese rayo velador que súbitamente te amenaza,
iluminando un instante tu frente desnuda,
para hundirse en tus ojos e incendiarte, abrasando
los espacios con tu vida que de amor se consume.

No. Esa luz que en el mundo
no es ceniza última,
luz que nunca se abate como polvo en los labios,
eres tú, poeta cuya mano y no luna
yo vi en los cielos una noche brillando.

Un pecho robusto que reposa atravesado por el mar
respira como la inmensa marea celeste
y abre sus brazos yacentes y toca, acaricia
los extremos límites de la tierra.

¿Entonces?
Si, poeta, arroja este libro que pretende encerrar en sus páginas un
        destello del sol,
y mira a la luz cara a cara, apoyada la cabeza en la roca,
mientras tus pies remotísimos sienten el beso postrero del poniente
y tus manos alzadas tocan dulce la luna,
y tu cabellera colgante deja estela en los astros.

FROM SOMBRA DEL PARAÍSO

And it isn't that alert lightning that jumps out,
throwing a quick light on your bare forehead
so it can sink into your eyes and set you on fire, blackening
space with your life, already eaten by love.

No. This light that isn't the final
burnt coal of the world,
that will never get depressed like dust on the lips,
that is what you are, poet, whose hand and not the moon
I saw shining in the sky one night.

A sturdy chest that lies covered by the sea
breathes like the immense tides of heaven,
and opens its resting arms to touch, to stroke
the farthest edges of the earth.

So then?
Go ahead, poet, get rid of this book, whose pages haven't caught the
    sun.
Go and look in the light, face to face, your head leaning on a rock,
while, far away, your feet feel the last kiss of the setting sun,
and your lifted hands softly brush the moon,
and your hanging hair leaves its wake among the stars.

TRANSLATED BY LEWIS HYDE

Ciudad del paraíso

A mi ciudad de Málaga

Siempre te ven mis ojos, ciudad de mis días marinos.
Colgada del imponente monte, apenas detenida
en tu vertical caída a las ondas azules,
pareces reinar bajo el cielo, sobre las aguas,
intermedia en los aires, como si una mano dichosa
te hubiera retenido, un momento de gloria, antes de hundirte para
     siempre en las olas amantes.

Pero tú duras, nunca desciendes, y el mar suspira
o brama por ti, ciudad de mis días alegres,
ciudad madre y blanquísima donde viví y recuerdo,
angélica ciudad que, más alta que el mar, presides sus espumas.

Calles apenas, leves, musicales. Jardines
donde flores tropicales elevan sus juveniles palmas gruesas.
Palmas de luz que sobre las cabezas, aladas,
mecen el brillo de la brisa y suspenden
por un instante labios celestiales que cruzan
con destino a las islas remotísimas, mágicas,
que allá en el azul índigo, libertadas, navegan.

Allí también viví, allí, ciudad graciosa, ciudad honda.
Allí, donde los jóvenes resbalan sobre la piedra amable,
y donde las rutilantes paredes besan siempre
a quienes siempre cruzan, hervidores, el brillos.

Allí fui conducido por una mano materna.
Acaso de una reja florida una guitarra triste
cantaba la súbita cancíon suspendida en el tiempo;

CITY OF PARADISE

For Málaga, my city

My eyes always return to you, city of my sea days.
Hanging from the high bluffs, your downward plunge
just barely stopped above the blue waves,
it seems you are the one who rules under the sky, over the water,
in the middle of the air, as if a joyful hand had held you up
for a moment of glory, before sinking you forever in the loving waves.

But you never go down, you survive, and the sea sighs
or bellows for you, city of my happy days,
white, white city where I once lived, mother I remember,
town that stands like an angel over the sea and rules its waves.

Little streets, airy and full of music. Gardens
with tropical flowers sending up their young, thick palms.
Palms full of light, like wings overhead, that stir up
the breeze's brightness and make the sky's lips pause
for a moment as they fly past, heading for
the most distant, magic islands that sail
wherever they please in the indigo blue.

I too lived in that soulful, lively city
where the young slide over the friendly rocks,
where the glittering walls will give a kiss
to everyone who keeps swarming past in the light.

A motherly hand led me from place to place.
Suspended in time, a sad guitar seemed to sing
the unexpected song of a flower-filled lattice.

quieta la noche, más quieto el amante,
bajo la luna eterna que instantánea transcurre.

Un soplo de eternidad pudo destruirte,
ciudad prodigiosa, momento que en la mente de un Dios emergiste.
Los hombres por un sueño vivieron, no vivieron,
eternamente fúlgidos como un soplo divino.

Jardines, flores. Mar alentando como un brazo que anhela
a la ciudad voladora entre monte y abismo,
blanca en los aires, con calidad de pájaro suspenso
que nunca arriba. ¡Oh ciudad no en la tierra!

Por aquella mano materna fui llevado ligero
por tus calles ingrávidas. Pie desnudo en el dia.
Pie desnudo en la noche. Luna grande. Sol puro.
Allí el cielo eras tú, ciudad que en él morabas.
Ciudad que en él volabas con tus alas abiertas.

FROM *SOMBRA DEL PARAÍSO*

The night was quiet and the suitor even quieter
under the momentary moon that flows by forever.

One breath of eternity could have destroyed you,
amazing city, passing thought in the mind of a god.
Men lived because of a dream, men didn't live,
they gave off light, forever, like a god's breath.

Gardens, flowers. The sea breathing like an arm that longs
for the city dangling between the cliffs and the abyss,
city as fine as a white bird that hangs in the air
and never lands. City that didn't come down!

The motherly hand took me lightly
through your weightless streets. Barefoot by day.
Barefoot by night. Full moon. Pure sun.
You were the sky and the sky was your home,
city that used to fly with your wings spread wide.

TRANSLATED BY LEWIS HYDE

Prose Interlude

Excerpts from "The Prologue to the Second Edition of *La destrucción o el amor*" by Vicente Aleixandre

"Vicente Aleixandre" by Pedro Salinas

"The Unknown Poet" by Vicente Aleixandre

EXCERPTS FROM "THE PROLOGUE TO THE SECOND EDITION OF *LA DESTRUCCIÓN O EL AMOR*" (1944)

VICENTE ALEIXANDRE

When did I begin to write? This question, invariably the first, is easily answered. I'm a rather late poet, if we call someone late who wasn't introduced to poetry until he was eighteen years old. Life went along until one summer, in a town in the Sierra de Avila where by chance we'd met and made friends, Dámaso Alonso, a boy like myself, handed me my first book of poems. How pleased I am to tell everybody now! The poet Dámaso gave me was Rubén Darío, and that truly maiden reading was a revolution to my soul. I discovered poetry: it stood revealed, and the one great passion of my life took hold in me, and never let go.

I had always been a boy who loved to read. But, no doubt like other Spanish boys back then, the only "poetry" I knew was the stuff in some miserable high school literature text which had taught me to loathe what seemed like a sterile, dull, and plodding form…

I couldn't wait to get out of classes and race to the National Library. But, my literature text in mind, I was careful never to ask for any poetry. When I was fourteen, sixteen, I read novels and plays insatiably. Many of our classic novels, almost all our nineteenth-century novels and a good number of the twentieth, plus a sizable chunk of seventeenth-century drama, made up the voracious reading of my adolescence. But I remember that in the drama I didn't *read* any of the verse—I was sorry it was verse. I wanted action, human complication, not language. The deadly memory of the textbook made me skip, for example, the sonnet-monologues, my impatient youth hurdling them with imaginative ease.

So at eighteen I was a young man saturated with reading, enthusiastic to the point of obsession about literature and its world of fantasy and passion, and ignorant, even wary, of poetry. When it made its sudden appearance, then, it was as something pure and untouched, something that grew and burned in a soul already experienced in the beauties of literature, but still innocent of the flash, sudden and complete, of poetic illumination...

Do they coincide, the moment a young man begins to write and the awakening of his creative life? For years I mixed my poems with my neglected schoolwork, writing them furtively, not telling anyone about them, never showing them to anyone. I was hardly the poet who feels he's been called, who knows what he wants and reaches out to it, meeting the future head on. I obeyed a primitive and confused instinct, powerful but almost impossible to talk about. I trembled in sweet agonies of pleasure. I treasured my poems as proof of an ardent but painful, because unsatisfying, struggle. No one ever saw my poems. This wasn't modesty. I realized later that it was fear of being hurt...

The awareness of actually being a poet—the consciousness of a real and possible calling—first came years later with the change stamped on the course of my life by a long and serious illness. Age: twenty-something. Solitude, country. Forced retirement from my first job with an industrial firm. Hours, an endless prospect of months, which grew into years, which were then my whole life, forever turned aside onto a different path. This total change decided my life. I wrote my first book. It was published...

I have written before, at various times and places, of my glimpses into poets and poetry. I will only repeat that for me the poet, the honest-to-God poet, is always one who reveals. The poet is essentially the seer, the prophet. But his "prediction" is not a prediction of the future; it might well be of the past: it is timeless prophecy. He illumines, he aims light, shakes men, he commands an "open sesame," a word that, in some mysterious way, can show them their destiny.

The poet is a man who might be more than a man: because he is a poet besides. The poet is full of "wisdom," but he can't feel proud because it may not be his: an unknowable force, a spirit speaks through his mouth. With his two feet planted on the earth, a mighty current forms, gathering beneath his soles, streaming through his body to leap from his tongue. It is thus the earth itself, the deep earth, that flames from that furious body. But other times the poet has climbed to the heights, and with his brow set among the heavens he speaks with the voice of the planets, with cosmic resonance, while in his breast he feels the very breath of the stars.

The tiny ant, the blade of soft grass under his cheek when he rests, are not different from himself. And he understands them, overhears their secret sound, which can just be made out amid the roar of thunder.

I don't believe that the poet is defined, at bottom, by his labor as a gold- or silversmith. The perfection of his work is a painstaking attention to craftsmanship, and his message is worth nothing if he offers men a rough or inadequate surface. But emptiness can never be redeemed by the patient toil of those who polish those sad metals.

Some poets—this is another matter, and not of expression, but rather of point of departure—are poets "of the few." They are artists (it makes no difference what stature) who address themselves to men by attending, so they say, to exquisite and narrow obsessions, to elegant trifles (what profound and delicate poems Mallarmé wrote to fans!), to distilled essences, expressive in miniature of our intricate civilization.

Other poets (again, stature makes no difference) address themselves to what is permanent in man. Not to the details that set us apart, but to the essence that brings us together. And while they see man caught up in his modern civilization, they also feel the pure nakedness radiating unchangeable from under his worn clothing. Love, sorrow, hatred, and death are changeless. These poets are radical poets and they speak to what is primordial, to what is elemental in humanity. They cannot *feel* themselves to be poets of the few. I am one of these.

TRANSLATED BY DAVID PRITCHARD

VICENTE ALEIXANDRE

PEDRO SALINAS

Vicente Aleixandre. No doubt about it. This strapping youth with the ruddy complexion, flushed and glowing, has just come from the playing field; all sweaty from the violent exercise, he must have given himself a good scrubbing under the shower.

And now, in street clothes, an elegant, stylish suit, with his jaunty step, he comes up to us flashing a smile so open, so friendly, there's no need to shake hands—the smile's taken care of all that. What does he play? Tennis? Rugby? Because only the constant rush of open air over the skin, and the excitement of a life spent leaping, chasing across a green field after something of no consequence whatsoever, could give a face this kind of utter epidermic joy.

"You must be kidding. Don't you know?"

Me? Know what?

Vicente is delicate, of very delicate health. He has to watch himself. For years now he's spent day after day lying quietly in the sun on a chaise longue in the garden behind his house. His parents dote on him and, to keep his spirits up, they've placed in front of him vast crystalline spaces of air, jagged peaks in the background, with touches of snow and incomparable blues: exactly, to the letter, like the Guadarrama mountains.

That's how Vicente's eyes, since they never see anything else, never watch anything but the shifting blue in the crystal air, got to be like that, so crystalline blue. He hardly ever goes anywhere! He never goes out after dark, period! When, on an occasional afternoon, Vicente makes it to one of those banquets we throw at Buenavista or the restaurant at the Frontón, we have a big celebration, we treat him like some mysterious traveler touching land for a few hours between two faraway shores. We find him the best spot, where there's no draft, we order him a special plate, and everyone tells him,

"Vicente, you look great, you look terrific!"

And he, like a schoolboy, can't stop smiling, he talks excitedly, and his little holiday is spent laughing and telling stories. He'll only stop smiling (if you ask me!) when, back in the quiet of his garden, in the mornings, while he's most alone, he shuts himself away—without moving, leaving his body as a pledge, lying there on the chaise longue—from the sun, the birds, from his blue eyes, and sinks into that troubled world of long mournful rhythms made of dreams of layered vegetation—heavenly woodlands, purgatorial forests, infernal thickets—where the purest trees cannot escape the vines that choke them, and are hopelessly entangled with the good love and the demented love in the emotions of men.

Because this strapping fellow, all smiles with us, so athletic in appearance, in reality fragile, this Vicente, delicate and apart, who never goes where people go, has discovered the most tragic form of equivalence: love equals desperation. And he spends his time—mathematical counter of his sorrow—figuring it out, in lyrical sums whose answer is always the same: love plus desperation equals poetry, deep, strangely moving poetry.

FROM *ENSAYOS DE LITERATURA HISPÁNICA*

TRANSLATED BY DAVID PRITCHARD

The Unknown Poet

Vicente Aleixandre

He came in wearing his uniform. He had called me the day before. "It's for you, some soldier." I had gone to the phone. "I'm a soldier, you know? And I've written two poems." I couldn't quite hear him. "What's that?" "Two poems, you know? It took a lot out of me." "What? What are you talking about?" "And I wanted to ask you—do you write night and day?" We were getting nowhere. After a couple more attempts, seeing how hard it was, we left it that he'd come by the next day. "But I can't say for sure I'll make it, you know? Because all I've got are these army clothes." In the end he agreed to come as he was.

And here he stood.

Sure enough, he was a soldier: with a badly wrinkled uniform, little bright staring eyes, a scrawny build under the baggy fit. "I'm from a town down in Huesca, you know?" He looked me over with that slow manner of country people who wouldn't be surprised at anything, who watch you half friendly, half stern. I saw right away that he was here for me to explain myself. He would ask the questions; my part was to answer him. "It takes a lot to write. It takes all you've got. I've written two poems," he told me again, "and it sure took a lot." He hadn't brought them. Apparently it didn't matter. Not writing them—*that* mattered, that took a lot. But showing them wasn't important—I don't think it had even occurred to him. He spoke with a certain dignity, not just common, but earthy. His face had something of dark crust about it, of earth, if not of bread. Wet clay put out to dry. This was a well-baked face. Like a fragment of adobe; maybe more like a piece of fallen roof tile, because it was long, thin, weathered, practically devoured by sun.

He stuck out his hand. "No, I didn't bring them. That would have been, you know…?" And again he asked that odd question: "Do you write night and day?" It was a little unsettling. I made him repeat it: "How do you mean, night and day?" Impatiently, his tolerance just keeping the edge, he clarified: "Do you write poems constantly?" I answered him truthfully (I almost put *humbly*): "Not night and day, no." "You mean, you don't write night and day? You don't write without stopping?" There was a terrific anxiety in his eyes, and back of that, a kind of threat. "Not exactly," I answered. "But then, you…" What a look he flashed me! A look of scorn, or better, of indignation, as if I'd had him fooled until now. "You…" that look was saying, "you're just like anybody. You write like anybody! Like me! And this is who they call a poet!"

The visit was over. He had suddenly understood that I was a man like himself, that writing, for me, could be a human endeavor, like for him. His look was no longer half friendly, half stern, but stern through and through. Because I'd fooled him. He got up. He made for the door. He hardly glanced at me on the way out. And he left, still full of faith in the poet as a god, redeemed from human cares, and dispenser of the magic formula that could "save" his chosen ones as well.

Because he, a soldier from some little Aragón village, forger of two poems that had taken labor and blood, had come to see the mighty being who poured poems out in an endless orgy, and who would save him too, lifting him to pure heights of infinite creation, merely saying "Do it" for the ascent to be done.

I closed the door, listening to his footsteps. He was the unknown poet and his faith moved mountains, brought them together. The waters in rivers flowed upstream and rejoiced in the freshness of the mountain springs. The sea stood still, the foaming wave hung in air, and someone moved dryshod over the pure shadow of water.

I looked out and saw him just turning the corner of the house. He was a kid, a soldier. And his body did the best it could inside the wrinkled uniform, several sizes too large.

FROM *LOS ENCUENTROS* (1954–1958)

TRANSLATED BY DAVID PRITCHARD

Poems with White Light

El viejo y el sol

Había vivido mucho.

Se apoyaba allí, viejo, en un tronco, en un gruesísimo tronco, muchas
    tardes cuando el sol caía.

Yo pasaba por allí a aquellas horas y me detenía a observarle.

Era viejo y tenía la faz arrugada, apagados, más que tristes, los ojos.

Se apoyaba en el tronco, y el sol se le acercaba primero, le mordía
    suavemente los pies

y allí se quedaba unos momentos como acurrucado.

Después ascendía e iba sumergiéndole, anegándole,

tirando suavemente de él, unificándole en su dulce luz.

¡Oh el viejo vivir, el viejo quedar, cómo se desleía!

Toda la quemazón, la historia de la tristeza, el resto de las arrugas, la
    miseria de la piel roída,

¡cómo iba lentamente limándose, deshaciéndose!

Como una roca que en el torrente devastador se va dulcemente
    desmoronando,

rindiéndose a un amor sonorísimo,

así, en aquel silencio, el viejo se iba lentamente anulando, lentamente
    entregando.

Y yo veía el poderoso sol lentamente morderle con mucho amor y
    adormirle

para así poco a poco tomarle, para así poquito a poco disolverle en
    su luz,

como una madre que a su niño suavísimamente en su seno lo
    reinstalase.

Yo pasaba y lo veía. Pero a veces no veía sino un sutilísimo resto.
    Apenas un levísimo encaje del ser.

Lo que quedaba después que el viejo amoroso, el viejo dulce, había
    pasado ya a ser la luz

THE OLD MAN AND THE SUN

He had lived a long time,
the old man said. In the evenings at sunset he used to rest there on the
        large, solid trunk of a fallen tree.
At the end of the day I'd pass that place and stop to look at him.
He was an old man with his face full of lines and his eyes dim, but
        not sad.
He rested on his log, and at first the sun drew close to him and gently
        nibbled at his feet—
then it seemed to curl up and rest for a while.
Soon it rose slowly and went flowing over him, flooding him,
pulling him gently toward it, making him whole in its sweet light.
As the old man lived, as he waited, how the sun thinned him out!
How slowly it burned away at the last wrinkles, his sad lined skin, the
        record of his misery,
how long it took, stripping and polishing everything!
In the silence the old man went slowly toward nothing, slowly
        surrendering himself,
the way a stone in a tumbling river gets sweetly abraded
and submits to the sound of pounding love.
And I saw the powerful sun slowly bite at him with great love, putting
        him to sleep
so as to take him bit by bit, so as to dissolve him with light bit by
        tiny bit,
the way a mother might bring her child very softly back to her breast.

I used to go by there and see him. But sometimes I could see nothing
        but a face made of air, just the lightest lacework of a person.
All that was left after the loving man, the kind old man, had passed
        over into light

y despaciosísimamente era arrastrado en los rayos postreros del sol,
como tantas otras invisibles cosas del mundo.

FROM *HISTORIA DEL CORAZÓN*

and was slowly, slowly pulled off in the last rays of the sun,
like so many other things we cannot see in this world.

Translated by Lewis Hyde

El sueño

Hay momentos de soledad
en que el corazón reconoce, atónito, que no ama.
Acabamos de incorporarnos, cansados: el día oscuro.
Alguien duerme, inocente, todavía sobre ese lecho.
Pero quizá nosotros dormimos... Ah, no: nos movemos.
Y estamos tristes, callados. La lluvia, allí insiste.
Mañana de bruma lenta, impiadosa. ¡Cuán solos!
Miramos por los cristales. Las ropas, caídas;
el aire, pesado; el aqua, sonando. Y el cuarto,
helado en este duro invierno que, fuera, es distinto.

Así te quedas callado, tu rostro en tu palma.
Tu codo sobre la mesa. La silla, en silencio.
Y sólo suena el pausado respiro de alguien,
de aquella que allí, serena, bellísima, duerme
y sueña que no la quieres, y tú eres su sueño.

FROM *HISTORIA DEL CORAZÓN*

146

THE DREAM

There are moments of loneliness
when the astonished heart realizes it feels no love.
We have just sat up, weary, the day dark.
Someone is still sleeping on that bed, like a child.
But maybe we are asleep… No: we're moving.
And we are sad, silent. Steady rain outdoors.
A morning of lazy, faithless fog. So alone!
We stare out the window. The clothes in a heap;
the heavy air; the drumming rain. And the room
icy in this hard winter which, outside, is something different.

So you keep quiet, your head in your hand.
Your elbow on the table. The chair, silence.
And the only sound is someone's slow breathing,
that woman who, serene and so beautiful, sleeps there
and dreams that you don't love her, and you are her dream.

TRANSLATED BY DEBORAH WEINBERGER

Mano entregada

Pero otro día toco tu mano. Mano tibia.
Tu delicada mano silente. A veces cierro
mis ojos y toco leve tu mano, leve toque
que comprueba su forma, que tienta
su estructura, sintiendo bajo la piel alada el duro hueso
insobornable, el triste hueso adonde no llega nunca
el amor. Oh carne dulce, que sí se empapa del amor hermoso.

Es por la piel secreta, secretamente abierta, invisiblemente entreabierta,
por donde el calor tibio propaga su voz, su afán dulce;
por donde mi voz penetra hasta tus venas tibias,
para rodar por ellas en tu escondida sangre,
como otra sangre que sonara oscura, que dulcemente oscura te besara
por dentro, recorriendo despacio como sonido puro
ese cuerpo, que ahora resuena mío, mío poblado de mis voces
    profundas,
oh resonado cuerpo de mi amor, oh poseído cuerpo, oh cuerpo sólo
    sonido de mi voz poseyéndole.

Por eso, cuando acaricio tu mano, sé que sólo el hueso rehúsa
mi amor—el nunca incandescente hueso del hombre—.
Y que una zona triste de tu ser se rehusa,
mientras tu carne entera llega un instante lúcido
en que total flamea, por virtud de ese lento contacto de tu mano,
de tu porosa mano suavísima que gime,
tu delicada mano silente, por donde entro
descacio, despacísimo, secretamente en tu vida,
hasta tus venas hondas totales donde bogo,
donde te pueblo y canto conpleto entre tu carne.

From Historia del corazón

HER HAND GIVEN OVER

One more day I touch your hand, your warm hand!
Your hand is thin and quiet—sometimes I shut
my eyes and stroke it gently, softly,
to feel its shape, to touch
its structure, the skin with its wings and beneath that
the stony bone that can't be bribed, the sad bone that never gets any
love. Oh sweet flesh that soaks itself in such splendid love!

The live heat spreads its voice, its gentle longing,
through your secret, hidden skin that starts to open;
and my voice slides through it into your warm blood
where it wanders, floating in your hidden streams
like a second blood singing a shadow song, dark like honey
it kisses you from within, flowing slowly like a clear tone in your body
that's an echo of my body now, my body full of strong voices.
Oh your echoing body wrapped around with just the sound of my
    voice!

So I know when I touch your hand only the bone refuses
my love—the never luminous human bone—.
And I know there's a sad layer in you that doesn't accept me
while your flesh comes white hot for a second,
coated with flame from that lazy stroking on your hand,
your silky, porous hand that begins to moan,
your fine, quiet hand where I come in
slowly, so slowly, secretly into your life,
down to all the deepest blood vessels where I float
and live and finish my song inside of you.

TRANSLATED BY LEWIS HYDE

Entre dos oscuridades, un relámpago

Y no saber adónde vamos, ni de dónde venimos.
—Rubén Darío

Sabemos adónde vamos y de dónde venimos. Entre dos oscuridades,
    un relámpago.
Y allí, en las súbita iluminación, un gesto, un único gesto,
una mueca más bien, iluminada por una luz de estertor.

Pero no nos engañemos, no nos crezcamos. Con humildad,
con tristeza, con aceptación, con ternura,
acojamos esto que llega. La conciencia súbita de una compañía, allí en
    el desierto.
Bajo una gran luna colgada que dura lo que la vida, el instante del
    darse cuenta entre dos infinitas oscuridades,
miremos este rostro triste que alza hacia nosotros sus grandes ojos
    humanos,
y que tiene miedo, y que nos ama.
Y pongamos los labios sobre la tibia frente y rodeemos
con nuestros brazos el cuerpo débil, y temblemos,
temblemos sobre la vasta llanura sin término donde sólo brilla la luna
    de estertor.

Como en una tienda de campaña
que el viento furioso muerde, viento que viene de las hondas profundi-
    dades de un caos,
aquí la pareja humana, tú y yo, amada, sentimos las arenas largas que
    nos esperan.
No acaban nunca, ¿verdad? En una larga noche, sin saberlo, las hemos
    recorrido;
quizá juntos, oh no, quizá solos, seguramente solos, con un invisible
    rostro cansado desde el origen, las hemos recorrido.

BETWEEN TWO NIGHTTIMES, LIGHTNING

And not knowing where we're going or where we came from.
—Rubén Darío

We know where we're going and where we came from. Between two
    nighttimes, lightning.
And there, in that short light, a face, a strange look,
more of a grimace, lit up by the light of a death rattle.

But let's not fool ourselves. Let's not be proud. Let's welcome what's
    coming
with humility, sorrow and resignation,
with tenderness. Suddenly it's clear we aren't alone out there in the
    wilderness.
Under a huge dangling moon that stays a lifetime, a moment of sight
    between two endless nights,
let's look at that sad face that lifts its big, human eyes toward us,
the face that's afraid and loves us.
And let's kiss that warm brow and encircle
the waning body in our arms. Then we'll tremble together
out there on the huge horizonless field where nothing shines but the
    moon of the death rattle.

As if in a tent
that the mad wind bites, a wind that flies up from the deep pits of
    chaos;
you and I, my love, the human couple, feeling the endless sand that
    waits all around us.
The sand never ends, does it? We came across it during the infinite
    night, without knowing;
we may have come together, no, more likely alone, certainly alone, each
    of our invisible faces tired out from the start.

Y después, cuando esta súbita luna colgada bajo la que nos hemos
    reconocido
se apague,
echaremos de nuevo a andar. No sé si solos, no sé si acompañados.
No sé si por estas mismas arenas que en una noche hacia atrás de
    nuevo recorreremos.

Pero ahora la luna colgada, la luna como estrangulada, un momento
    brilla.
Y te miro. Y déjame que te reconozca.
A ti, mi compañía, mi sola seguridad, mi reposo instantáneo, mi
    reconocimiento expreso donde yo me siento y me soy.
Y déjame poner mis labios sobre tu frente tibia—oh, cómo la siento—.
Y un momento dormir sobre tu pecho, como tú sobre el mío,
mientras la instantánea luna larga nos mira y con piadosa luz nos
    cierra los ojos.

From Historia del corazón

And later when that quick, hanging moon that let us know each other
goes out,
then we'll start walking again. Alone or with someone else, I don't
    know.
Maybe back over the same sand that we'll walk on again one night, I
    don't know.

But for now the hanging moon, as if strangled, flares up for a moment.
And I look at you; you let me come closer.
And here where I wake and live I'm grateful to you my companion, my
    one sure thing, my moment of rest.
And let me put my lips on your warm face—it feels so good!—
And let me fall asleep awhile on your breast, and you on mine,
while the fleeting full moon watches us and, with its light of pity, closes
    our eyes.

Translated by Lewis Hyde

Después del amor

Tendida tú aquí, en la penumbra del cuarto,
como el silencio que queda después del amor,
yo asciendo levemente desde el fondo de mi reposo
hasta tus bordes, tenues, apagados, que dulces existen.
Y con mi mano repaso las lindes delicadas de tu vivir retraído
y siento la musical, callada verdad de tu cuerpo, que hace un instante,
    en desorden, como lumbre cantaba.
El reposo consiente a la masa que perdió por el amor su forma
    continua,
para despegar hacia arriba con la voraz irregularidad de la llama,
convertirse otra vez en el cuerpo voraz que en sus límites se rehace.

Tocando esos bordes, sedosos, indemnes, tibios, delicadamente
    desnudos,
se sabe que la amada persiste en su vida.
Momentánea destrucción el amor, combustión que amenaza
al puro ser que amamos, al que nuestro fuego vulnera,
sólo cuando desprendidos de sus lumbres deshechas
la miramos, reconocemos perfecta, cuajada, reciente la vida,
la silenciosa y cálida vida que desde su dulce exterioridad nos llamaba.
He aquí el perfecto vaso del amor que, colmado,
opulento de su sangre serena, dorado reluce.
He aquí los senos, el vientre, su redondo muslo, su acabado pie,
y arriba los hombros, el cuello de suave pluma reciente,
la mejilla no quemada, no ardida, cándida en su rosa nacido,
y la frente donde habita el pensamiento diario de nuestro amor, que
    allí lúcido vela.
En medio, sellando el rostro nítido que la tarde amarilla caldea sin
    celo,

AFTER LOVE

As you lie there in the shadows of the room,
like the silence that stays after making love,
I, from the depths of my half-sleep, rise lightly toward
your faint, shadowed borders that still exist, so sweet.
And with my hand I stroke the delicate outer boundary of your with-
    drawn life,
I feel the hushed, musical truth of your body that only a moment ago
    sang like a disordered fire.
And your half-sleep allows the clay—which lost its lasting form in the
    act of love,
which leapt up like a hungry, ragged flame—
to turn itself back again into the true body that remakes itself in its own
    limits.

Touching the warm edges of a lover's body—silky, unhurt,
delicately naked—we know that her life will go on.
Love is a momentary destruction, a combustion that threatens
the pure creature we love, the one who's wounded in our fire.
But after we've pulled away from her unraveled flames
and looked at her, we see clearly the new, re-formed and flawless life,
the quiet, warm life that called to us from the sweet surface of her body.
Here is love's perfect vessel, filled
and overflowing with its serene and glistening golden blood.
Here are the breasts, the belly, her rounded thigh, her foot below
and her shoulders above, her neck like a soft new feather,
her cheek neither scorched nor burnt, but frank with its new rosy flush,
and her brow where the daily thought of our love makes its home and
    keeps watch with clear eyes.
And at the center, sealing her silhouetted face which the yellow evening
    warms without a fuss,

está la boca fina, rasgada, pura en las luces.

Oh temerosa llave del recinto del fuego.

Rozo tu delicada piel con estos dedos que temen y saben,

mientras pongo mi boca sobre tu cabellera apagada.

FROM *HISTORIA DEL CORAZÓN*

lies her mouth, torn, pure in the light.
Modest entry to the storehouse of fire!
With these fingers, afraid and aware, I stroke your delicate skin
while, with my mouth, I begin again to cover your cooling hair.

TRANSLATED BY LEWIS HYDE

LA EXPLOSIÓN

Yo sé que todo esto tiene un nombre: existirse.
El amor no es el estallido, aunque también exactamente lo sea.
Es como una explosion que durase toda la vida.
Que arranca en el rompimiento que es conocerse y que se abre, se abre,
se colorea como una ráfaga repentina que, trasladada en el tiempo,
se alza, se alza y se corona en el transcurrir de la vida,
haciendo que una tarde sea la existencia toda, major dicho, que toda la
     existencia sea como una gran tarde,
como una gran tarde toda del amor, donde toda
la luz se diría repentina, repentina en la vida entera,
hasta colmarse en el fin, hasta cumplirse y coronarse en la altura
y allí dar la luz completa, la que se despliega y traslada
como una gran onda, como una gran luz en que los dos nos
     reconociéramos.

Toda la minuciosidad del alma la hemos recorrido.
Sí, somos los amantes que nos quisiéramos una tarde.
La hemos recorrido, ese alma, minuciosamente, cada día sorpren-
     diéndonos con un espacio más.
Lo mismo que los enamorados de una tarde, tendidos,
revelados, van recorriendo su cuerpo luminoso, y se absorben,
y en una tarde son y toda la luz se da y estalla, y se hace,
y ha sido una tarde sola del amor, infinita,
y luego en la oscuridad se pierdan, y nunca ya se verán, porque nunca
     se reconocerían…

THE EXPLOSION

I know all this has a name: to be given life.
Love isn't a bomb bursting, though at the same time that's really what
 it is.
It's like an explosion that lasts a whole lifetime.
It comes out of that breakage they call knowing yourself, and then it
 opens wider and wider,
colored like a quick cloud of sunlight that rolls through time
and floats up and up until it ripens in the passage of life,
so that an afternoon becomes all existence, or better: all existence is
 like one long afternoon,
like a roomy afternoon full of love, where
all the light in the universe suddenly gathers, suddenly in a whole
 lifetime,
until at last it's full, it's all formed and ripened at the top
and from there the fullest light comes down, the light that unrolls and
 unfolds
like a huge wave, like a huge light that lets us look on each other at last.

We've gone all over the soul's smallest details.
Yes, we're the lovers who fell in love one afternoon.
We've gone over that soul so slowly, always surprised to find it still
 larger in the morning.
The same way that afternoon lovers, lying there,
uncovered, go over and over their glowing body, absorbed in
 themselves,
and in that afternoon all the light comes out and bursts and grows,
and it's been an endless afternoon of love,
and then later they're lost in the dark, and now they'll never see each
 other again, they'd never recognize each other...

Pero esto es una gran tarde que durase toda la vida. Como tendidos,
nos existimos, amor mío, y tu alma,
trasladada a la dimension de la vida, es como un gran cuerpo
que en una tarde infinita yo fuera reconociendo.
Toda la tarde entera del vivir te he querido.
Y ahora lo que allí cae no es el poniente, es sólo
la vida toda lo que allí cae; y el ocaso
no es: es el vivir mismo el que termina,
y te quiero. Te quiero y esta tarde se acaba,
tarde dulce, existida, en que nos hemos ido queriendo.
Vida que toda entera como una tarde ha durado.
Años como una hora en que he recorrido tu alma,
descubriéndola despacio, como minuto a minuto.
Porque lo que allí está acabando, quizá, sí, sea la vida.
Pero ahora aquí el estallido que empezó se corona
y en el colmo, en los brillos, toda estás descubierta,
y fue una tarde, un rompiente, y el cenit y las luces
en alto ahora se abren de todo, y aquí estás: ¡nos tenemos!

FROM *HISTORIA DEL CORAZÓN*

But ours is a long afternoon that lasts a lifetime. We give each other
    life,
as if we were lying down and your soul, my love,
shifted into this life-place, is like a huge body
that I devoted myself to one endless afternoon.
I've loved you every moment of that afternoon.
And now, that isn't the sunset falling over there, that's
all of life falling; and that isn't
the sun sinking; it's life itself coming to an end,
and I love you. I love you and this afternoon is ending,
this luxurious, breathing afternoon where we've been making love.
A life gone by all together like an afternoon.
The years were just an hour during which I've gone into your soul,
slowly uncovering it, minute by minute.
Because what's just finishing over there could be life, *is* life.
But the first flash is finishing here and now
and you're fully revealed in the ripening and the sparks,
and it was an afternoon, a breaking wave, and the summit and the
    lights
at the top are all open now, and you're here and we have each other!

Translated by Lewis Hyde

Comemos sombra

Todo tú, fuerza desconocida que jamás te explicas.
Fuerza que a veces tentamos por un cabo del amor.
Allí tocamos un nudo. Tanto así es tentar un cuerpo,
un alma, y rodearla y decir: "Aquí está." Y repasamos despaciosamente,
morosamente, complacidamente, los accidentes de una verdad que
      únicamente por ellos se nos denuncia.
Y aquí está la cabeza, y aquí el pecho, y aquí el talle y su huida,
y el engolfamiento repentino y la fuga, las dos largas piernas dulces que
      parecen infinitamente fluir, acabarse.
Y estrechamos un momento el bulto vivo.

Y hemos reconocido entonces la verdad en nuestros brazos, el cuerpo
      querido, el alma escuchada,
el alma avariciosamente aspirada.

¿Dónde la fuerza entonces del amor? ¿Dónde la replica que nos diese
      un Dios respondiente,
un Dios que no se nos negase y que no se limitase a arrojarnos un
      cuerpo, un alma que por él nos acallase?
Lo mismo que un perro con el mendrugo en la boca calla y se obstina,
así nosotros, encarnizados con el duro resplandor, absorbidos,
estrechamos aquello que una mano arrojara.
Pero ¿dónde tú, mano sola que haría
el don supremo de suavidad con tu piel infinita,
con tu sola verdad, única caricia que, en el jadeo, sin términos nos
      callase?

Alzamos unos ojos casi morbundos. Mendrugos,
panes, azotes cólera, vida, muerte:

WE FEED ON SHADOW

Every bit of you, mysterious power that never explains yourself.
You, force we sometimes feel with the thread of love.
There's the snag. That's what it is to feel a body,
a soul, to surround it and say: "Here it is." And slowly, very slowly
and with pleasure we examine a truth that shows us nothing but its
    inessentials:
here's the head and here's the breast, here's the waist and its escape
    route,
and the sudden swamping and the flight, the two long sweet legs that
    appear to be forever flowing, finishing.
And for a moment we clutch that lump of life.
And then we've recognized the truth in our arms, the desired body, the
    overheard soul,
the soul we covet with such greed.

After that, where's the force of love? Where's the answer a responsive
    God would have given us,
a God who wouldn't have denied himself to us, who wouldn't have just
    thrown us a body, a soul, to keep us quiet?
Just the way a dog with a scrap in its mouth will shut up and won't let
    go,
that's like us, bloodied with the harsh splendor, full of it,
we clutch what a hand seems to have thrown us.
But where are you, the only hand that could give
the supreme gift, the softness of your undying skin,
of your one truth, the only caress that might have kept us quiet,
    panting, forever?

We lift up our eyes from the edge of death. Table scraps,
crusts of bread, beatings, rage, life, death:

todo lo derramas como una compasión que nos dieras,
como una sombra que nos lanzaras, y entre los dientes nos brilla
un eco de un resplandor, el eco de un eco de un eco del resplandor,
y comemos.
Comemos sombra, y devoramos el sueño o su sombra, y callamos.
Y hasta admiramos: cantamos. El amor es su nombre.

Pero luego los grandes ojos húmedos se levantan. La mano
no está. Ni el roce
de una veste se escucha.
Sólo el largo gemido, o el silencio apresado.
El silencio que sólo nos acompaña
cuando, en los dientes la sombra desvanecida, famélicamente de nuevo
echamos a andar.

FROM *HISTORIA DEL CORAZÓN*

you pour it all out like a gift of compassion,

like a shadow you've thrown to us, and an echo of a splendor shines

between our teeth, the echo of an echo of an echo of the splendor,

and we eat it.

We eat the shadow, we feed on the dream or its shadow, and we quiet
 down.

And we even admire it: we sing. Its name is Love!

But once more the huge, damp eyes lift up. There isn't

any hand. Not even

the rustle of garments.

Only the long lamentation, or the tightly held silence.

The silence that goes with us only

when—with the shadow fading in our teeth—we set out on foot again,
 full of hunger.

TRANSLATED BY LEWIS HYDE

Mirada final

(Muerte y reconocimiento)

La soledad, en que hemos abierto los ojos.
La soledad en que una mañana nos hemos despertado, caídos,
derribados de alguna parte, casi no pudiendo reconocernos.
Como un cuerpo que ha rodado por un terraplén
y, revuelto con la tierra súbita, se levanta y casi no puede reconocerse.
Y se mira y se sacude y ve alzarse la nube de polvo que él no es, y ve
      aparecer sus miembros,
y se palpa: "Aquí yo, aquí mi brazo, y éste mi cuerpo, y ésta mi pierna, e
      intacta está mi cabeza";
y todavía mareado mira arriba y ve por dónde ha rodado,
y ahora el montón de tierra que le cubriera está a sus pies y él emerge,
no sé si dolorido, no sé si brillando, y alza los ojos y el cielo destella
con un pesaroso resplandor, y en el borde se sienta
y casi siente deseos de llorar. Y nada le duele,
pero le duele todo. Y arriba mira el camino,
y aquí la hondonada, aquí donde sentado se absorbe
y pone la cabeza en las manos; donde nadie le ve, pero un cielo azul
      apagado parece lejanamente contemplarle.

Aquí, en el borde del vivir, después de haber rodado toda la vida como
      un instante, me miro.
¿Esta tierra fuiste tú, amor de mi vida? ¿Me preguntaré así cuando en el
      fin me conozca, cuando me reconozca y despierte,
recién levantado de la tierra, y me tiente, y sentado en la hondonada,
      en el fin, mire un cielo piadosamente brillar?

Final Look

(Death and Recognition)

Loneliness, in which we have opened our eyes.
Loneliness, in which we awaken one morning, fallen,
thrown down from somewhere, almost unable to recognize ourselves.
Like a body which has rolled down an embankment
and, covered with the sudden earth, stands up and almost can't recog-
　　nize himself.
And he looks at himself and dusts himself off and he sees arise the
　　cloud of dust which he is not, and he sees his limbs appear,
and he touches himself: "Here I am, here is my arm, and this is my
　　body, this my leg, and my head's intact";
and, still dizzy, he looks up and sees where he has rolled,
and now the pile of dirt that covered him is at his feet and he
　　emerges—
I don't know if aching or if shining—and he raises his eyes and sees
　　the sky sparkle
with a sorrowful radiance, and he sits on the edge
and almost feels like crying. And nothing hurts,
but everything hurts. And he looks at the road above,
and the ravine here below, here where he sits lost in thought
resting his head in his hands; where nobody sees him, but a dull blue
　　sky seems to gaze at him from afar.

Here, on the edge of living, after rolling down my whole life like an
　　instant, I look at myself.
Were you on this earth, love of my life? Will I ask myself this when at
　　the end I know myself, when I recognize myself, and I awake,
newly risen from the earth, and I touch myself, and sitting in the
　　ravine, at the end, I look at a sky shining with mercy?

No puedo concebirte a ti, amada de mi existir, como sólo una tierra
    que se sacude al levantarse, para acabar cuando el largo rodar de
    la vida ha cesado.
No, polvo mío, tierra súbita que me ha acompañado todo el vivir.
No, material adherida y tristísima que una postrer mano, la mía
    misma, hubiera al fin de expulsar.
No: alma más bien en que todo yo he vivido, alma por la que me fue la
    vida possible
y desde la que también alzaré mis ojos finales
cuando con estos mismos ojos que son los tuyos, con los que mi alma
    contigo todo lo mira,
contemple con tus pupilas, con las solas pupilas que siento bajo los
    párpados,
en el fin cielo piadosamente brillar.

FROM *HISTORIA DEL CORAZÓN*

I cannot conceive of you, love of my existence, as merely earth which
    shakes itself upon arising, only to end when the long spinning of
    life has ceased.

No, my dust, sudden earth which has been with me throughout life.

No, clinging matter so sad which a last hand, my very own, must
    finally throw off.

No: soul, rather, in which all of me has lived, soul which made my life
    possible

and from which too I shall raise my final eyes

when, with these same eyes which are yours, eyes through which my
    soul looks at everything with you,

in the end I will gaze with your eyes, the only eyes I feel beneath my
    lids,

at the sky shining with mercy.

TRANSLATED BY DEBORAH WEINBERGER

El visitante

Aquí también entré, en esta casa.
Aquí vi a la madre cómo cosía.
Una niña, casi una mujer (alguien diría: qué alta, qué guapa se está
    poniendo),
alzó sus grandes ojos oscuros, que no me miraban.
Otro chiquillo, una menuda sombra, apenas un grito, un ruidillo por el
    suelo,
tocó mi piernas suavamente, sin verme.
Fuera, a la entrada, un hombre golpeaba, confiado, en un hierro.

Y entré, y no me vieron.
Entré por una puerta, para salir por otra.

Un viento pareció, mover aquellos vestidos.

Y la hija alzó su cara, sus grandes ojos vagos y llevó a su frente sus
    dedos.

Un suspiro profundo y silencioso exhaló el pecho de la madre.

El niño se sintió cansado y dulcemente cerró los ojos.

El padre detuvo su maza y dejó su mirada en la raya azul del
    crepúsculo.

FROM *HISTORIA DEL CORAZÓN*

THE VISITOR

I too came into this house.
And here I saw the mother sewing.
A girl, almost a woman (someone might say: how tall, how attractive
    she's becoming),
looked up, but her large, dark eyes passed through me.
A little boy, a mere shadow, a squeak, a half-grown noise on the floor,
softly touched my legs, without seeing me.
Out in the dooryard a man was beating methodically on a piece of
    iron.

I came in, but they didn't see me.
I came in one door only to go out another.

A breeze seemed to move their clothing.

And the daughter lifted her face, her wide eyes drifting, and put her
    fingers to her forehead.

From deep in her bosom the mother heaved a quiet sigh.

The boy felt sleepy and gently closed his eyes.

The father paused with his sledge and rested his eyes on the blue line
    of twilight.

TRANSLATED BY SHEPHERD BLISS

En la plaza

Hermoso es, hermosamente humilde y confiante, vivificador y
    profundo,
sentirse bajo el sol, entre los demás, impelido,
llevado, conducido, mezclado, rumorosamente arrastrado.

No es bueno
quedarse en la orilla
como el malecón o como el molusco que quiere calcáreamente imitar a
    la roca.
Sino que es puro y sereno arrasarse en la dicha
de fluir y perderse,
encontrándose en el movimiento con que el gran corazón de los hom-
    bres palpita extendido.

Como ése que vive ahí, ignoro en qué piso,
y le he visto bajar por unas escaleras
y adentrarse valientemente entre la multitude y perderse.
La gran masa pasaba. Pero era reconocible el diminuto corazón afluido.
Allí, ¿quién lo reconocería? Allí con esperanza, con resolucíon o con fe,
    con temeroso denuedo,
con silenciosa humildad, allí él también
transcurría.

Era una gran plaza abierta, y había olor de existencia.
Un olor a gran sol descubierto, a viento rizándolo,
un gran viento que sobre las cabezas pasaba su mano,
su gran mano que rozabo las frentes unidas y las reconfortaba.

Y era el serpear que se movía
como un único ser, no sé si desvalido, no sé si poderoso,
pero existente y perceptible, pero cubridor de la tierra.

In the Square

It's beautiful, beautifully simple and sure, deeply exhilarating,
to find yourself out in the sun, in the crowd, lifted
and carried, caught up and pushed and pulled along in the noise.

It's so good
to stay at the edge
like a seawall or a mollusk that tries, in its limy way, to look like a stone.

It's better, pure and easy, to surrender yourself to the delight
of flowing, getting lost, finding
yourself in the rhythm of the huge human heart that beats all around
   you.

Like the man who lives somewhere up in that building.
I've seen him come down the stairs
and go bravely into the multitude, and disappear.
The huge crowd was moving past. And yet it was felt when his small
   heart joined them.
He was there—who could feel it?—with his hope, with his faith or
   determination, his cautious bravery,
his quiet humility—he was there too,
on his way.

It was a large, open square and it smelled of life.
It smelled of the great revealed sunlight, of a wind that rippled it,
a big wind that stroked their heads with its hand, a big hand
that brushed the crowd of faces and left them reassured.

And, as if it were a single creature, the crowd
snaked along—helpless? powerful? I don't know—
but it existed, you could see it, it covered the earth.

Allí cada uno puede mirarse y puede alegrarse y puede reconocerse.
Cuando, en la tarde caldeada, solo en tu gabinete,
con los ojos extraños y la interrogación en la boca,
quisieras algo preguntar a tu imagen,

no te busques en el espejo,
en un extinto diálogo en que no te oyes.
Baja, baja despacio y búscate entre los otros.
Allí están todos, y tú entre ellos.
Oh, desnúdate y fúndete, y reconócete.

Entra despacio, como el bañista que, temeroso, con mucho amor y
    recelo al agua,
introduce primero sus pies en la espuma,
y siente el agua subirle, y ya se atreve, y casi ya se decide.
Y ahora con el agua en la cintura todavía no se confía.
Pero él extiende sus brazos, abre al fin sus dos brazos y se entrega
    completo.
Y allí fuerte se reconoce, y crece y se lanza,
y avanza y levanta espumas, y salta y confía,
y hiende y late en las aguas vivas, y canta, y es joven.

Así, entra con pies desnudos. Entra en el hervor, en la plaza.
Entra en el torrente que te reclama y allí sé tú mismo.
¡Oh pequeño corazón diminuto, corazón quiere latir
para ser él también el unánime corazón que le alcanza!

FROM *HISTORIA DEL CORAZÓN*

You can find yourself in the crowd, you can see your own face there
     and feel the sadness fall away.
If you're alone in your study on some hot afternoon,
with your puzzled eyes and a question on the tip of your tongue,
and if you'd like to ask your reflection for the answer,

don't go holding dead, voiceless discussions
with the mirror. Go down,
go down slowly and seek yourself among the others.
Everyone is there and you are with them.
Take off your clothes! Get in and see what you're like!

Don't hurry. Go in like a cautious swimmer who has such wary love
     for the water
that at first he only puts his feet in the waves.
Then he feels the water rise, he gets his nerve, he's almost decided.
The water comes up to his waist, but still he doesn't trust it.
But he reaches out at last, at last he spreads his arms and gives in
     completely.
And he realizes his own strength; he grows, he shoves off,
he pushes forward, leaping, kicking up waves and trusting it.
He cuts through the living water, in rhythm with it, singing and young.

So take off your shoes and go in. Go into the swarming square.
Go and discover your own face in the torrent that claims you.
Small, miniature heart! Blood that longs to beat
and become one with the harmonious heart that soaks it up!

Translated by Lewis Hyde

Al colegio

Yo iba en bicicleta al colegio.
Por una apacible calle muy céntrica de la noble ciudad misteriosa.
Pasaba ceñido de luces, y los carruajes no hacían ruido.
Pasaban majestuosos, llevados por nobles alazanes o bayos, que
     caminaban con eminente porte.
¡Cómo alzaban sus manos al avanzar, señoriales, definitivos,
no desdeñando el mundo, pero contemplándolo
desde la soberana majestad de sus crines!
Dentro, ¿qué? Viejas señoras, apenas poco más que de encaje,
chorreras silenciosas, empinados peinados, viejísimos terciopelos:
silencio puro que pasaba arrastrado por el lento tronco brillante.

Yo iba en bicicleta, casi alado, aspirante.
Y había anchas aceras por aquella calle soleada.
En el sol, alguna introducida mariposa volaba sobre los carruajes y
     luego por las aceras
sobre los lentos transeúntes de humo.
Pero eran madres que sacaban a sus niños más chicos.
Y padres que en oficinas de cristal y sueño...
Yo al pasar los miraba.
Yo bogaba en el humo dulce, y allí la mariposa no se extrañaba.
Pálida en la irisada tarde de invierno,
se alargaba en la despaciosa calle como sobre un abrigado valle
     lentísimo.
Y la vi alzarse alguna vez para quedar suspendida
sobre aquello que bien podía ser borde ameno de un río.
Ah, nada era terrible.
La céntrica calle tenía una posible cuesta y yo ascendía, impulsado.

On the Way to School

I rode my bicycle to school.
Along a peaceful street that ran through the center of the noble, myste-
  rious city.
I rode by, surrounded by lights, and the carriages made no noise.
They passed, majestic, pulled by distinguished bays or chestnuts that
  moved with a proud bearing.
How they lifted their hooves as they went along, like gentlemen,
  precise,
not disdaining the world, but studying it
from the sovereign grace of their manes!
And inside, what? Old ladies, scarcely a little more than lace,
silent ornaments, stuck-up hairstyles, ancient velvet:
a pure silence passing, pulled by the heavy shining animals.

I rode my bicycle, I almost had wings, I was inspired.
And there were wide sidewalks along that sunny street.
In the sunlight, some sudden butterfly hovered over the carriages and
  then, along the sidewalks,
over the slow strollers made of smoke.
But they were mothers taking their littlest children for a walk.
And fathers who, in their offices of glass and dreams...
I looked as I went by.
I sailed through the sweet smoke, and the butterfly was no stranger.
Pale in the iridescent winter afternoon,
she spread herself out in the slow street as over a sheltered, sleepy
  valley.
And I saw her swept up sometimes to hang suspended
over what could as well have been the pleasant bank of a river.
Ah, nothing was terrible.
The street had a slight grade and up I went, driven on.

Un viento barría los sombreros de las viejas señoras.
No se hería en los apacibles bastones de los caballeros.

Y encendía como una rosa de ilusión, y apenas de beso, en las mejillas
    de los inocentes.
Lós árboles en hilera era un vapor inmóvil, delicadamente
suspenso bajo el azul. Y yo casi ya por el aire,
yo apresurado pasaba en mi bicicleta y me sonreía...
y recuerdo perfectamente
cómo misteriosamente plegaba mis alas en el umbral mismo del
    colegio.

FROM *HISTORIA DEL CORAZÓN*

A wind swept the hats of the old ladies.

It wasn't hurt by the peaceful canes of the gentlemen.

And it lit up like an imaginary rose, a little like a kiss, on the cheeks of
the children.

The trees in a row were a motionless vapor, gently

suspended under the blue. And by now nearly up in the air,

I hurried past on my bicycle and smiled...

and I remember perfectly

how I folded my wings mysteriously on the very threshold of the
school.

TRANSLATED BY STEPHEN KESSLER

La clase

Como un niño que en la tarde brumosa va diciendo su lección y se
   duerme.
Y allí sobre el magno pupitre está el mudo profesor que no escucha.
Y ha entrado en la última hora un vapor leve, porfiado,
pronto espesísimo, y ha ido envolviéndolos a todos.
Todos blandos, tranquilos, serenados, suspiradores,
ah, cuán verdaderamente reconocibles.
Por la mañana han jugado,
han quebrado, proyectado sus límites, sus ángulos, sus risas, sus
   imprecaciones, quizá sus lloros.
Y ahora una brisa inoíble, una bruma, un silencio, casi un beso, los
   une,
los borra, los acaricia, suavísimamente los recompone.
Ahora son como son. Ahora puede reconocérseles.
Y todos en la clase se han ido adurmiendo.
Y se alza la voz todavía, porque la clase dormida se sobrevive.
Una borrosa voz sin destino, que se oye y que no se supiera ya de quién
   fuese.

Y existe la bruma dulce, casi olorosa, embriagante,
y todos tienen su cabeza sobre la blanda nube que los envuelve.
Y quizá un niño medio se despierta y entreabre los ojos,
y mira y ve también el alto pupitre desdibujado
y sobre él el bulto grueso, casi de trapo, dormido, caído,
del abolido profesor que allí sueña.

FROM Historia del corazón

THE CLASS

Like a boy in the hazy afternoon who
goes on saying his lesson as he falls asleep.
And there, over the huge front desk, is the speechless professor who
    isn't listening.
During the last hour a light, persistent haze has entered
and, suddenly thick, it's wrapped itself around everyone.
Soft, calm, pacified, breathing, oh—
how truly familiar they are!
All morning they've played,
they broke through, shot their limits, their angles, their laughter, their
    curses, maybe even their tears.
And now an inaudible breeze, a mist, a silence, a kiss almost, gathers
    them together,
erases them, caresses them, and very gently mends them.
Now they are as they are. Now they can be recognized.
And everyone in the class has been falling asleep.
And, because the class lives on as it sleeps, the voice keeps rising;
no one knew whose it was anymore, though they could all hear it, a
    blurred and aimless voice.

And the sweet haze is real, intoxicating, a little fragrant,
and all of them rest their heads on the soft, enveloping cloud.
And one boy may wake a little, open his eyes a crack,
and look up to see the high, blurry desk
with that fleshy bulk draped across it, a sort of rag pile, asleep and
    fallen—
the obliterated professor who is dreaming in front of the class.

TRANSLATED BY LEWIS HYDE

El niño y el hombre

A José A. Muñoz Rojas

I

El niño comprende al hombre que va a ser,
y callándose, por indicios, nos muestra, como un padre, al hombre que
   apenas todavía se puede adivinar.
Pero él lo lleva, y lo conduce, y a veces lo desmiente en sí mismo,
   valientemente, como defendiéndolo.
Si mirásemos hondamente en los ojos del niño, en su rostro inocente y
   dulce,
veríamos allí, quieto, ligado, silencioso,
al hombre que después va a estallar, al rostro experimentado y duro, al
   rostro espeso y oscuro
que con una mirada de desesperación nos contempla.

Y nada podemos hacer por él. Está reducido, maniatado, tremendo.
Y detrás de los barrotes, a través de la pura luz de la tranquila pupila
   dulcísima,
vemos la desesperación y el violento callar, el cuerpo crudo y la mirada
   feroz,
y un momento nos asomamos con sobrecogimiento
para mirar el cargado y tapiado silencio que nos contempla.

Sí. Por eso vemos al niño con descuidada risa perseguir por el parque
   el aro gayo de rodantes colores.
Y le vemos despedir de sus manos los pájaros inocentes.
Y pisar unas flores tímidas tan levemente que nunca estruja su viviente
   aromar.
Y dar gritos alegres y venir corriendo a nosotros, y sonreírnos

THE BOY AND THE MAN

For José A. Muñoz Rojas

I

Inside the small boy is the man he will become.

Without a word he makes the signs, like a father, that show us the man
he'll be, hardly visible now.

But he carries that man, he leads him around and sometimes hides
him inside of himself as if he were a brave watchman.

If we look way down in the boy's eyes, into his innocent and pretty
face,

we see him there, never moving, quiet, trapped.

We see the man who's going to break out, we see the hard face of a
man who's lived a long time, a thick, dark face

that stares back at us in desperation.

And we can't do a thing for him. He is held back, his hands tied.
Frightening.

And through the cage, through the clear light from that sweet still eye,

we can see his desperation, his violent silence, his rough body and
wild-animal eyes,

and for a moment we're surprised—it worries us

to see this constrained and electric silence staring at us.

Yes. That's why we see the boy chase his bright hoop of spinning color
through the park with a careless laugh.

And we see him let innocent birds fly out of his hands.

And walk through the bashful flowers so lightly that he never bruises
their living odor.

And shout joyfully and come running up and smile at us

con aquellos ojos felices donde sólo apresuradamente miramos,
oh ignorantes, oh ligeros, la ilusión de vivir y la confiada llamada a los
    corazones.

II

Oh, niño, que acabaste antes de lo que nadie esperaba,
niño que, con una tristeza infinita de los que te rodaban, acabaste en la
    risa.
Estás tendido, blanco en tu dulzura póstuma,
y un rayo de luz continuamente se abate sobre tu cabeza dorada.

En un momento de soledad yo me acerco.
Rubio el bucle inocente, externa y tersa aún
la aterciopelada mejilla inmóvil,
un halo de quietud pensativa y vigilante
en toda tu actitud de pronto se me revela.

Yo me acerco y te miro. Me acerco más y me asomo.
Oh, sí, yo sé bien lo que tú vigilas.
Niño grande, inmenso, que cuidas celosamente al que del todo ha
    muerto.
Allí está oculto, detrás de tuz grandes ojos,
allí en la otra pieza callada. Allí, dormido, desligado, presente.
Distendido el revuelto ceño, caída la innecesaria mordaza rota.
Aflojado en su secreto sueño, casi dulce en su terrible cara en reposo.

Y al verdadero meurto, al hombre que definitivamente no nació,
el niño vigilante calladamente bajo su apariencia lo vela.
Y todos pasan, y nadie sabe que junto a la definitiva soledad del hondo
    muerto en su seno,
un niño pide silencio con un dedo en los labios.

FROM *Historia del corazón*

with those merry eyes. And we (so ignorant and careless!)
look hastily in at life's illusion and the trusting appeal to our hearts.

II

Little boy, you were done before anyone expected.
Child, you finished in laughter, leaving everyone around you with an
      endless sadness.
Now you're laid out, pale with the sweetness that comes after death,
and all the time a beam of light is thrown on your golden head.

When we're alone for a moment I move close to you.
Your innocent hair is blond, your velvet, motionless cheek is still
      smooth and pudgy.
Suddenly I can see the halo of thoughtful,
vigilant calm around your body.

I go closer and watch. Even closer, and look in.
Ah yes, I know what it is you're protecting.
Big boy, huge child, you're jealously guarding the one who really died.
He is hidden in there, on the other side of your large eyes,
there in that other, quiet chamber. There in the present, asleep and set
      free.
The overturned frown has stretched out, the needless, broken muzzle
      has fallen off.
Released into his secret dream, this terrible face is almost pretty now
      that it's at rest.

And beneath his own face the watchful boy quietly takes care
of the one who's really dead, the man who was never born at all.
And the people go by the boy, lying beside the true loneliness of a
      death sunk inside of him,
and no one sees him putting a finger to his lips, asking us to be quiet.

TRANSLATED BY LEWIS HYDE

El moribundo

A Alfonso Costafreda

I
Palabras

El decía palabras.
Quiero decir palabras, todavía palabras.
Esperanza. El Amor. La Tristeza. Los Ojos.
Y decía palabras,
mientras su mano ligeramente débil sobre el lienzo aún vivía.
Palabras que fueron alegres, que fueron tristes, que fueron soberanas.
Decía moviendo los labios, quería decir el signo aquél;
el olvidado, ése que saben decir mejor dos labios,
no, dos bocas que fundidas en soledad pronuncian.
Decía apenas un signo leve como un suspiro, decía un aliento,
una burbuja; decía un gemido y enmudecían los labios,
mientras las letras teñidas de un carmín en su boca
destellaban muy débiles, hasta que al fin cesaban.

Entonces alguien, no sé, alguien no humano,
alguien puso unos labios en los suyos.
Y alzó una boca donde sólo quedó el calor prestado,
las letras tristes de un beso nunca dicho.

THE MAN ON HIS DEATH BED

For Alfonso Costafreda

I
Words

He was saying words.
I mean to say words, more words.
Hope. Love. Sadness. The Eyes.
And all the time his gently weak hand was alive on the bed linen
he kept on talking.
The words had been happy, or they'd been sad, or dignified.
His lips moved as he spoke. He wanted to say that unique word,
the one we've forgotten, the one meant for two lips to speak,
or rather: the one that two mouths say when they're pressed together
    in loneliness.
What he spoke was just barely a sign, airy like a breath. He spoke a
    breeze,
a bubble: he spoke a groan and then nothing,
while the letters, now stained scarlet in his mouth,
shone very weakly and went out.

Then someone else, I don't know who, someone who wasn't human
someone pressed two lips against his lips.
And a mouth floated up leaving nothing there but the borrowed heat,
the sad letters of a kiss that never got spoken.

II

El silencio

Miró, miró, por último y quiso hablar.
Unas borrosas letras sobre sus labios aparecieron.
Amor. Sí, amé. He amado. Amé, amé mucho.
Alzó su mano débil, su mano sagez, y un pájaro
voló súbito en la alcoba. Amé mucho, el aliento aún decía.
Por la ventana negra de la noche las luces daban su claridad
sobre una boca, que no bebía ya de un sentido agotado.
Abrió los ojos. Llevó su mano al pecho y dijo:
Oídme.
Nadie oyó nada. Una sonrisa oscura veladamente puso su dulce
    máscara
sobre el rostro, borrándolo.
Un soplo sonó. Oídme. Todos, todos pusieron su delicado oído.
Oídme. Y se oyó puro, cristalino, el silencio.

FROM *NACIMIENTO ÚLTIMO*

II
The Silence

He lay there watching at the end, he watched and wanted so much to
    speak.
Some faded letters appeared over his lips.
Love. Yes, I was in love. I've loved. I loved so much.
He lifted his frail, wise hand and suddenly
a bird was flying in the bedroom. His breath kept saying, I loved so
    much.
Outside the black, night window the lights sent a glow
over his mouth that had stopped drinking from that worn-out life.
He opened his eyes. He put his hand to his chest and said:
Listen to me!
No one could hear a thing. A strange smile lowered its smooth mask
    like a veil
over his face, rubbing it out.
There was a little wind. Listen to me! Everyone, everyone strained their
    delicate ears.
Listen! And they heard it—pure and crystal tone—the silence.

TRANSLATED BY LEWIS HYDE

Para quién escribo

I

¿Para quién escribo?, me preguntaba el cronista, el periodista o simplemente el curioso.

No escribo para el señor de la estirada chaqueta, ni para su bigote enfadado, ni siquiera para su alzado índice admonitorio entre las tristes ondas de música.

Tampoco para el carruaje, ni para su ocultada señora (entre vidrios, como un rayo frío, el brillo de los impertinentes).

Escribo acaso para los que no me leen. Esa mujer que corre por la calle como si fuera a abrir las puertas a la aurora.

O ese viejo que se aduerme en el banco de esa plaza chiquita, mientras el sol poniente con amor le toma, le rodea y le deslíe suavemente en sus luces.

Para todos los que no me leen, los que no se cuidan de mí, pero de mí se cuidan (aunque me ignoren).

Esa niña que al pasar me mira, compañera de mi aventura, viviendo en el mundo.

Y esa vieja que sentada a su puerta ha visto vida, paridora de muchas vidas, y manos cansadas.

Escribo para el enamorado; para el que pasó con su angustia en los ojos; para el que le oyó; para el que al pasar no miró; para el que finalmente cayó cuando preguntó y no le oyeron.

Who I Write For

I

Historians and newsmen and people who are just curious ask me, Who
    am I writing for?

I'm not writing for the gentleman in the stuffy coat, or for his offended
    moustache, not even for the warning finger he raises in the sad
    ripples of music.

Not for the lady hidden in her carriage (her lorgnette sending its cold
    light through the windowpanes).

Perhaps I write for people who don't read my poems. That woman
    who dashes down the street as if she had to open the doors for
    the sunrise.

Or that old fellow nodding on a bench in the little park while the set-
    ting sun takes him with love, wraps him up and dissolves him,
    gently, in its light.

For everyone who doesn't read my writing, all the people who don't
    care about me (though they care for me, without knowing).

The little girl who glances my way as she passes, my companion on this
    adventure, living in the world.

And the old woman who sat in her doorway and watched life and bore
    many lives and many weary hands.

I write for the man who's in love. For the man who walks by with his
    pain in his eyes. The man who listened to him. The man who
    looked away as he walked by. The man who finally collapsed when
    he asked his question and no one listened.

Para todos escribo. Para los que no me leen sobre todo escribo. Uno a
    uno, y la muchedumbre. Y para los pechos y para las bocas y para
    los oídos donde, sin oírme,
está mi palabra.

II

Pero escribo también para el asesino. Para el que con los ojos cerrados
    se arrojó sobre un pecho y comió muerte y se alimentó, y se
    levantó enloquecido.

Para el que se irguió como torre de indignación, y se desplomó sobre el
    mundo.

Y para las mujeres muertas y para los niños muertos, y para los hom-
    bres agonizantes.

Y para el que sigilosamente abrió las llaves del gas y la ciudad entera
    pereció, y amaneció un montón de cadáveres.

Y para la muchacha inocente, con su sonrisa, su corazón, su tierna
    medalla, y por allí pasó un ejército de depredadores.

Y para el ejército de depredadores, que en una galopada final fue a
    hundirse en las aguas.

Y para esas aguas, para el mar infinito.

Oh, no para el infinito. Para el finito mar, con su limitación casi
    humana, como un pecho vivido.

(Un niño ahora entra, un niño se baña, y el mar, el corazón del mar,
    está en ese pulso.)

Y para la mirada final, para la limitadísima Mirada Final, en cuyo seno
    alguien duerme.

I write for all of them. I write, mostly, for the people who don't read
    me. Each one and the whole crowd. For the breasts and the
    mouths and the ears, the ears that don't listen, but keep
my words alive.

II

But I also write for the murderer. For the man who shut his eyes and
    threw himself at somebody's heart and ate death instead of food
    and got up crazy.

For the man who puffed himself up into a tower of rage and then col-
    lapsed on the world.

For the dead woman and the dead children and dying men.

For the person who quietly turned on the gas and destroyed the whole
    city and the sun rose on a pile of bodies.

For the innocent girl with her smile, her heart, her sweet medallion
    (and a plundering army went through there).

And for the plundering army that charged into the sea and sank.

And for the waters, for the infinite sea.

No, not infinite. For the finite sea that has boundaries almost like our
    own, like a breathing lung.

(At this point a little boy comes in, jumps in the water, and the sea, the
    heart of the sea, is in his pulse!)

And for the last look, the hopelessly limited Last Look, in whose arms
    someone falls asleep.

Todos duermen. El asesino y el injusticiado, el regulador y el naciente,
  el finado y el húmedo, el seco de voluntad y el híspido como
  torre.

Para el amenazador y el amenazado, para el bueno y el triste,
para la voz sin materia
y para toda la materia del mundo.

Para ti, hombre sin deificación que, sin quererlas mirar, estás leyendo
  estas letras.

Para ti y todo lo que en ti vive,
yo estoy escribiendo.

FROM EN UN VASTO DOMINIO

Everyone's asleep. The murderer and the innocent victim, the boss and
the baby, the damp and the dead, the dried-up old fig and the
wild, bristling hair.

For the bully and the bullied, the good and the sad,
the voice with no substance
and all the substance of the world.

For you, the man with nothing that will turn into a god, who reads
these words without desire.

For you and everything alive inside of you,
I write, and write.

Translated by Lewis Hyde

A MI PERRO

Oh, sí, lo sí, buen "Sirio", cuando me miras con tus grandes ojos pro-
fundos.
Yo bajo a donde tú estás, o asciendo a donde tú estás
y en tu reino me mezclo contigo, buen "Sirio", buen perro mío, y me
salvo contigo.
Aquí en tu reino de serenidad y silencio, donde la voz humana nunca
se oye,
converso en el oscurecer y entro profundamente en tu mediodía.
Tú me has conducido a tu habitación, donde existe el tiempo que
nunca se pone.
Un presente continuo preside nuestro diálogo, en el que el hablar es el
tuyo tan sólo.
Yo callo y mudo te contemplo, y me yergo y te miro. Oh, cuán profun-
dos ojos conocedores.
Pero no puedo decirte nada, aunque tú me comprendes...Oh, yo te
escucho.
Allí oigo tu ronco decir y saber desde el mismo centro infinito de tu
presente.
Tus largas orejas suavísimas, tu cuerpo de soberanía y de fuerza,
tu ruda pezuña peluda que toca la materia del mundo,
el arco de tu aparición y esos hondos ojos apaciguados
donde la Creación jamás irrumpió como una sorpresa.
Allí, en tu cueva, en tu averno donde todo es cenit, te entendí, aunque
no pude hablarte.
Todo era fiesta en mi corazón, que saltaba en tu derredor, mientras tú
eras tu mirar entendiéndome.
Desde mi sucederse y mi consumirse te veo, un instante parado a tu
vera,
pretendiendo quedarme y reconocerme.
Pero yo pasé, transcurrí y tú, oh gran perro mío, persistes.

To My Dog

Yes, it's clear to me, good Sirius, whenever you look at me with your
   big, thoughtful eyes.
I come down here where you live—or I come up—
and join you in your kingdom where you save me, my good dog Sirius.
Here in your calm and quiet world where there are no human voices
I chat with you in the evening; I go straight to the middle of your day.
You've brought me to your home where there's a kind of time that has
   no sunsets.
An unending present stands over our conversation. You're the only one
   who talks,
I fall silent and look at you as if I'd lost my voice. I sit up and watch.
   Your eyes are so thoughtful and wise!
But even though you'd understand, there's nothing for me to say…
   I just listen.
I hear your hoarse speech and wisdom rise from the boundless core of
   the present.
Your long, incredibly soft ears, your strong proud body,
your rough, shaggy paws in touch with the material world,
the curve of your silhouette and those calm, unfathomed eyes
where the Creation never breaks in to upset you.
There in your cave, in your dark hole full of light, I knew what you
   meant though I couldn't speak.
My heart swelled with joy and went bounding around you (while you
   kept giving me that knowing look).
From my expansion and exhaustion I can see you, pausing a moment
   at your side,
trying to stop and figure me out.
But I kept going, I went on while you stayed, my big friend.

Residido en tu luz, inmóvil en tu seguridad, no pudiste más que enten-
derme.

Y yo salí de tu cueva y descendí a mi alvéolo viajador, y, al volver la
cabeza, en la linde.

vi, no sé, algo como unos ojos misericordes.

From Retratos con nombre

You live in your own light, your security doesn't change, the best you
    could do for me was understand.
And I left your cave and went down to my little traveler's compart-
    ment. And when I turned my head at the border
I could see—what was it?—something like the eyes of pardon.

Translated by Lewis Hyde

Materia humana

Y tú que en la noche oscura has abierto los ojos y te has abierto los
  ojos y te has levantado.
Te has asomado a la ventana.
La ciudad en la noche. ¿Qué miras? Todos van lejos.
Todos van cerca.
Todos muy juntos en la noche. Y todos y cada uno en su ventana, única
  y múltiple.

Si tú mueves esa mano, la ciudad lo registra un instante y vibra en las
  aguas.
Y si tú nombras y miras, todos saben que miras, y esperan y la ciudad
  recibe la onda pura de una materia.
Toda la ciudad común se ondea y la ciudad toda es una materia:
una onda única en la que todos son, por la que todo es, y en la que
  todos están; llegan, pulsan, se crean.
Onda de la materia pura en la que inmerso te hallas, que por ti existe
  también y que desde lejísimos te ha alcanzado.
Allí respira en la extensión total—¡ah, humanidad!—con toda su
  dimensión profunda casi infinita.

Ah, qué inmenso cuerpo posees.
Toda esa materia que viene del fondo del existir,
que un momento se detiene en ti y sigue tras ti, propagándote y
  heredándote y por la que tú significadamente sucedes.
Todo es tu cuerpo inmenso, como el de aquel, como el de ese otro,
  como el de aquella niña, como el de aquella vieja,
como el de aquel guerrero que no se sabe, allá en el fondo de las
  edades, y que está latiendo contigo.
Contigo el emperador y el soldado, el monje y el anacoreta. Contigo
la cortensana pálida que acaba de ponerse su colorete en la triste

Human Matter

And you in the dark night who've opened your eyes and risen.
You've gone to the window and looked out.
The city at night. What do you see? Everyone far away.
Everyone near.
Everyone so close together in the night. And all and each one in win-
    dows, singular and many.

If you move your hand, the city feels it for an instant, and a wave
    begins in the water.
And if you speak and look, everyone knows you're watching, and they
    wait, and the city receives a pure wave of substance.
The whole common city ripples and the whole city is all one substance:
a single wave where everyone is, where everything is, and where all
    exist; they arrive, their hearts beat, they come alive.
A pure material wave where you find yourself immersed, to which you
    too give life, and which has reached you from a long way off.
There, humanity expands and breathes, extended in space, almost
    limitless.

You have such a huge body!
All that matter rising from the depths of existence,
which pauses in you a moment and then goes on, generating you and
    inheriting you and giving your existence meaning.
It's all your own immense body, as it is his body, and another's body,
    and that little girl's, and that old woman's,
as it is that warrior's who doesn't know himself, there in the depths of
    the ages, beating along with you.
With you the emperor and the soldier, the monk and the hermit. With
    you
the pale courtesan who's just finished painting her sad, spent cheek.

mejilla, ah, cuán gastada. Allí en la infinitud de los siglos.

Pero aquí sonríe contigo, bracea en la onda de la materia pura, y late
  en la virgen.

Como ese gobernante sereno que fríamente condena, allá en la lejan-
  ísima noche, y respira ahora también en la boca pura de un niño.

Todos confiados en la vibración sola que a todos suma,

o mejor, que a todos compone y salva, y hace y envía, y allí

se pierde todavía íntegra hacia el futuro.

Oh, todo es presente.

Onda única en extensión que empieza en el tiempo, y sigue y no tiene
  edad

O la tiene, sí, como el Hombre.

FROM EN UN VASTO DOMINIO

There in the endless centuries.
But here she smiles with you, she swims in the swell of the pure matter,
     and her heart beats inside the virgin.
Like that calm governor who coldly condemns, there in the far-off
     night, and breathes now in the pure mouth of a child.
Everyone trusting the single vibration which sums them all up,
or better, supports and saves them, carries and makes them, and there,
still whole, is losing itself in the future.

Everything's present.

A single wave spread out which begins in time, and continues and has
     no age.
Or has one, yes, like Man.

TRANSLATED BY STEPHEN KESSLER

La sangre

Mas si el latido empuja
sangre y en oleadas lentas va indagando,
va repartiendo,
por los brazos, hasta afinarse en yema;
por las piernas hasta tocar la tierra,
casi la tierra,
sin alcanzarla nunca
(una frontera, apenas una lámina,
separa linfa y tierra, destinadas a unirse
pero mucho más tarde.
Oh bodas diferidas, mas seguras).

Digo que si el latido empuja
y por el brazo llega al externo, y va alegre,
refrescando, otorgando,
con nueva juventud y se diría
que con nueva esperanza...
cuando vuelve va oscura
—sangre apagada y triste de los hombres—
sombra que por sus túneles regresa
a su origen continuo.

¿Cuál es su carga?, dime.
Llegó a la mano y ésta
ahora soltaba el puño del arado,
o depuso una pluma,
o venía de enjugar la frente húmeda,
para lo cual el hierro
activo—azada o pala o filo—
quedó un instante en sombra

Blood

Let's say the heart pumps
the blood in slow, enormous waves, and it goes
searching, giving itself
all down the arms, right out to the fingertips;
down through the legs until it almost touches
the earth,
though it never quite makes it—(because
there's a border, just a thin sheet
between lymph and earth, which are meant to be
together, but not for a long time yet.
That wedding is put off—but it will come!)

What I'm saying is, if the heartbeat shoves it
out the whole length of the arm, and it flows
refreshingly, free with its blessings, joyous
and full of new youth, perhaps even
new hope ... still,
its return is a dark run—
the sad, extinguished blood of men—
a shadow shuddering back through its tunnels, back
to its constant beginning.

Tell me, what does it carry?
It comes into the hand, which now
loosens its grip on the plow,
or lays the pen aside,
or drops from wiping the sweating forehead dry,
while the laboring
metal—machete or shovel or hoe—
rests a moment in the shade.

El riego alegre recogió la carga,
todo el conocimiento del esfuerzo oscuro,
y emprendió su regreso.
¡Sangre cargada de la ciencia humana!
Hacia arriba, despacio,
como un inmenso lastre se adentraba
más en el hombre. Primero por su brazo,
sabio de su dolor, luego en su hombro:
¡cómo pesaba inmensa!
Luego, por su camino horizontal buscando a ciegas
el descanso, la fuente,
el manantial de luz, de vida: el fresco
pozo donde lavar su oscura túnica
y levantarse nueva, suavemente empujada,
suavemente creída, como oreada,
para emprender de nuevo, sin memoria,
su dulce
curiosidad,
su indagación primera, su sorpresa, su firme y pura y honda
esperanza diaria.

Es la verdad que algunas veces en la boca aún destella
y se hace
una palabra humana.

FROM *En un vasto dominio*

Then the bright canals gather in the cargo,
all that dense knowledge of dark exertion,
and start it back toward the heart.
Blood laden with human knowledge!
Slowly, slowly it rises
like an immense ballast forcing its way deeper and deeper
into the man. First through his arm
that knows about pain; then into his shoulder:
what an impossible weight!
At last, searching blindly along the horizontal path
for its resting place,
the fountain, the source
of light, of life: the fresh
well where it will wash its dark tunic and
rise up new—gently pushed along,
lightly innocent as a breeze—to take up
once more, without memory,
its sweet
curiosity,
its first exploration, its surprise, its pure and firm and deep
daily hope.

The truth is that sometimes, from inside the mouth, it still scatters rays
    of light
and makes
a human word.

TRANSLATED BY TOMÁS O'LEARY

LA OREJA—LA PALABRA

I

Ese dibujo acaso
interroga. Mas si así es lo traza
con materia indudable.
Cartílago irrumpiente que surte repentino
como un pabellón noble.
Oh, sí, interroga al mundo
y el mundo da el tañido, hace su cristalina afirmación,
y él la recoge entera.
El mundo no es la masa,
aunque tenga su música.
No es el dibujo exacto de la risa o la furia,
aunque todo haga un son.
Rugosa, apresurada, revuelta, no indecisa,
la oreja se ha formado por siglos de paciencia,
por milenios de enorme voluntad esperando.
Y allí espiaba acaso su percepción más justa,
su verdad más precisa.
La transustanciación no visible
a que asciende
el mundo, en asunción
de sí, y se alza a su música.
Se espía a sí mismo por ese órgano noble,
hecho materia sólo, sentido sólo, espíritu:
mundo entero compacto.

Y el cartílago avanza casi animal y casi
mineral y se asoma.
Por el diestro agujero

The Ear—The Word

I

Maybe the shape of it
is asking a question. And if so it's outlined
with a substance that isn't open to doubt.
Cartilage, that breaks out with a sudden spurt
like a royal pavilion.
Yes, it inquires of the world
and the world gives back a tone, saying "yes" with crystal,
and the ear gathers it all in.
The world is not that lump,
although it has its music.
Rage and laughter aren't the real shape of the ear,
although everything makes a sound.
Wrinkled and hurried, intricate but not hesitant,
the ear has been formed by centuries of patience,
by a million years of enormous and hopeful willpower.
Maybe it's been trying to catch its most accurate observation,
its most precise truth.
The world has risen!—
an invisible transubstantiation—
it has climbed up
itself and come into its own music.
It lies waiting for itself in that royal organ,
made of nothing but matter, nothing but feeling, spirit:
a whole, tight world.

And the cartilage—part animal and part mineral—
comes forward and looks out.
It pokes out of its handy hole

irrumpe, se contrae, se arruga se dispone,
se consolida y abre
su ala clara y quietísma.
Y allí aguarda, Allí goza
el mundo. Allí se escucha
el mundo. Y son los hombres
los que traducen luego con su signo o palabras
la respuesta a la Vida.

II

La palabra responde, por el mundo. Hay mañanas
en que oímos el mar, la tierra en ella.
Es una cueva oscura, o un relámpago fijo.
Noches que se iluminan con la palabra humana.
¡Un firmamento o voz!
Pero a veces, muchas más veces, la palabra limita
con el hombre, es el hombre. La palabra gimiendo,
la palabra escuchando. ("Dime, amor".) La palabra
escupiendo, apostrofando, reuniendo.
Clamando como sólo una ardiente campana
fundida y aún colgante, vibrando, reclamando,
mientras todos los hombres a su voz se concentran,
y hay un coro de brazos, de puños proferidos,
una voz, y son todos.

La palabra es un hilo
de voz, y es una madre.
Y es un niño esperando.
Y es un padre en su fragua.
Y es un carbón brillando.
Y es un hogar que ardiendo quema las voluntades,
y nace el hombre nuevo.

and then shrinks and wrinkles,
it gets settled and firm
and opens up its clear, quiet wing.
And there it waits. There it enjoys
the world. There the world listens
to itself. And later men are the ones
who use its sign or words
to figure out the answer to Life.

II

The word answers, for the world. There are mornings
we hear the sea inside of it, or the earth.
It's a shadowy cave or a suspended lightning bolt.
Some nights are lit up with the words of people.
A voice or a starry sky!
But sometimes, most of the time, the words stop
with man, they are man. The complaining word,
the listening word ("Say something, sweetheart"). The word
spitting and calling names and making friends.
Crying out loud like a lonesome bell, melted in its own fire
and still hanging, shaking and complaining,
while everyone on earth tries to hear its voice
and there is a choir of arms, and fists speaking up,
and all of them, one voice.

The word is one thread
of the voice, and it is a mother.
And it is a waiting child.
And a father at his forge.
And a glowing piece of charcoal.
And it is a fireplace where all willfulness burns up
and the man is born again.

Palabra de los hombres que hace al fin un domingo.
Muchachas que descienden de las lomas queridas,
de las muy esperadas.
Muchachos que les dicen palabras como auroras,
como besos redondos,
besos como horizonte o palabras cantadas.
Palabra o coro cierto con las manos prendidas,
rodando, oh sí, girando
en el diáfano día.

From En un vasto dominio

The words of men, that finally add up to a Sunday.
The young women, who come down from the hills we love,
the hills, we've waited for so long.
The young men, who tell them words like sunrises
or like round kisses,
kisses like the horizon or chanted words.
The word or the true choir holding hands
and wheeling around, yes, spinning
through the translucent sunlight.

TRANSLATED BY LEWIS HYDE

LA MUERTE DEL ABUELO

Pasé de puntillas
y todavía se oía el penoso alentar del enfermo.

Y me senté en mi cuarto de niño,
y me acosté
Se oía en la casa entrar y salir, y allá en el fondo,
como un murmullo, el largo rumor de la mar que rodaba.

Soñé que él y yo paseábamos en una barca.
¡Y cómo cogíamos peces! Y qué hermoso estaba el mar terso.
Y qué fresco vientecillo bajo el sol largo.
Él tenía la misma cara bondadosa de siempre,
y con su mano me enseñaba los brillos,
las vaporosas costas felices, las crestitas del agua.
Y qué feliz en la barca solo con él...
Solo con él, tan grande y tan seguro para mí allí; solo con él en el mar.
"¡No lleguemos tan pronto!" ..., dije. Y él se reía.
Tenía el cabello blanco, como siempre, y aquellos ojos azules que dicen
      que son los míos.
Y me empezó a contar un cuento. Y yo empecé a dormirme.
Ah, allí mecido en el mar. Con su voz que empujaba.
Me dormí y soñé su voz. Ah, el sueño en el sueño...
Y soñé que soñaba. Y muy dentro otro sueño. Y más dentro otro, y
      otro,
y yo más hondo soñándole, con él al lado, y huyendo los dos sueño
      adentro.

Y de pronto, la barca...Como si tropezase.

MY GRANDFATHER'S DEATH

I went by on tiptoe
and could still hear the painful breathing of the sick man.

And I sat down in my little-boy's room,
and I went to bed.
I could hear people entering and leaving the house, and way in the back-
    ground,
like a murmur, the long sound of the tossing sea.

I dreamed that he and I were out in a boat.
And what fish we caught! And how beautiful the smooth sea was.
And what a fresh breeze under the long sunlight.
He had the same kind face as always,
and with his hand he pointed out the sparkles,
the hazy happy coastline, the little crests of water.
And how happy I was alone with him in the boat...
Alone with him, so big and so secure for me out there; alone with him
    on the sea.
"Let's not get there so soon!"..., I said. And he laughed.
He had white hair, as always, and those blue eyes they tell me I have too.
And he started to tell me a story. And I started to fall asleep.
Ah, rocked out there on the sea. With his voice pushing us along.
I slept and I dreamed his voice. A dream within a dream...
And I dreamed I was dreaming. And way inside, another dream. And
    deeper another, and another,
and I at the bottom dreaming him, with him beside me, and both of us
    flying further into the dream.

And suddenly the boat... As if it struck something.

Ah, sí, ¡cómo abrí ojos! (Y nadie, y mi cuarto.)
Y había un silencio completo como de arribo.

FROM *POEMAS VARIOS*

I opened my eyes! (And no one, just my room.)
And there was an utter silence as of arrival.

TRANSLATED BY STEPHEN KESSLER

En la muerte de Miguel Hernández

I

No lo sé. Fue sin música.
Tus grandes ojos azules
abiertos se quedaron bajo el vacío ignorante,
cielo de la losa oscura,
masa total que lenta desciende y te aboveda,
cuerpo tú solo, inmenso,
único hoy en la Tierra,
que contigo apretado por los soles escapa.

Tumba estelar que los espacios ruedas
con sólo él, con su cuerpo acabado.
Tierra caliente que son sus solos huesos
vuelas así, desdeñando a los hombres.
¡Huye! ¡Escapa! No hay nadie;
sólo hoy su inmensa pesantez de sentido,
Tierra, a tu giro por los astros amantes.
Sólo esa Luna que en la noche aún insiste
contemplará la montaña de vida.
Loca, amorosa, en tu seno le llevas,
Tierra, oh Piedad, que sin mantos le ofreces.
Oh soledad de los cielos. Las luces
sólo su cuerpo funeral hoy alumbran.

II

No, ni una sola mirada de un hombre
ponga su vidrio sobre el mármol celeste.
No le toquéis. No podríais. Él supo,

On the Death of Miguel Hernández

I

I don't know. There wasn't any music.
Your wide, blue eyes
stayed open under the ignorant atmosphere,
the clouded, gravestone sky,
utter, sluggish mass that pushes down, arching over
you, corpse alone, immense,
the only one left on Earth today
as she escapes through the stars with you in her arms.

You drift through the fields of stars, tomb
with his burned-out body and nobody else.
Warm-blooded Earth, you carry his solitary bones,
you fly off with them, turning your back on mankind.
Get away! Escape! There's no one here;
nothing, today, but the great heaviness of his heart
as you, Earth, spin through the loving stars.
Nothing but that Moon who still insists on staying up
all night to keep her eye on the mountain of his life.
Crazy, full of love, you carry him on your breast,
Earth, oh Mercy! that you hold him up without a veil.
The heavens are so lonely! Today the lights
give light to nothing but his body, ready for the grave.

II

No, don't let a single human eye
put its glass over the sky-borne slab.
Don't touch him. None of you could. He knew,

sólo él supo. Hombre tú, sólo tú, padre todo
de dolor. Carne sólo para amor. Vida sólo
por amor. Sí. Que los ríos
apresuren su curso: que el agua
se haga sangre: que la orilla
su verdor acumule: que el empuje
hacia el mar sea hacia ti, cuerpo augusto,
cuerpo noble de luz que te diste crujiendo
con amor, como tierra, como roca, cual grito
de fusion, como rayo repentino que a un pecho
total único del vivir acertase.

Nadie, nadie. Ni un hombre. Esas manos
apretaron día a día su garganta estelar. Sofocaron
ese caño de luz que a los hombres bañaba.
Esa gloria rompiente, generosa que un día
revelara a los hombres su destino; que habló
como flor, como mar, como pluma, cual astro.
Sí, esconded, esconded la cabeza. Ahora hundidla
entre tierra, una tumba para el begro pensamiento cavaos,
y morded entre tierra las manos, las uñas, los dedos
con que todos ahogasteis su fragante vivir.

III

Nadie gemirá nunca bastante.
Tu hermoso corazón nacido para amar
murió, fue muerto, muerto, acabado, cruelmente acuchillado de odio.
¡Ah! ¿Quién dijo que el hombre ama?
¿Quién hizo esperar un día amor sobre la tierra?
¿Quién dijo que las almas esperan el amor y a su sombra florecen?
¿Quién su melodioso canto existe para los oídos de los hombres?
Tierra ligera, ¡vuela!

only he knew. Only you, you man, father full
of sorrow. Flesh only for love. Life only
out of love. Yes. Let the rivers
hasten their course: let the water
turn to blood: let the riverbank
thicken its foliage: let the rush
toward the sea be toward you, stately body,
body raised up with its own light, crackling
with love, like dirt, like stones or a cry
of fusion, like a streak of light that might have hit
life in its complete and singular heart.

No one, no one. Not one man. Those hands
squeezed his starry throat, day after day. They choked
that stream of light that used to bathe mankind.
That bursting, generous glory that might have
shown us our destiny one day; that spoke
like flower, like sea, like feather or a star.
Yes hide, bury your heads. Sink them
in the ground now, dig a tomb for your own black thoughts,
and eat away your hands, your nails, the fingers
all of you used to smother the fragrant way he lived.

III

No one could ever grieve enough.
Your beautiful heart was born to love
and died, was dead, dead, finished, cruelly hacked by hate.
Oh, who said that men feel love?
Who made us hope that love might come down one day?
Who said our souls wait for it, that they will flower in its shade?
That it sings its harmony for the ears of men?
Nimble earth, fly!

Vuela tú sola y huye.
Huye así de los hombres, despeñados, perdidos,
ciegos restos del odio, catarata de cuerpos
crueles que tú, bella, desdeñando hoy arrojas.

Huye hermosa, lograda,
por el celeste espacio con tu tesoro a solas.
Su pesantez, al seno de tu vivir sidéreo
da sentido, y sus bellos miembros lúcidos para siempre
inmortales sostienes para la luz sin hombres.

FROM *Cuadernos de las horas situadas*

Fly off by yourself, get away.
Leave mankind behind, discarded, lost,
the blind remains of hate, waterfall of cruel
bodies that you throw off today, turning your lovely face away.

Fly through celestial space,
beautiful, fulfilled, all alone with your treasure.
His heaviness brings its heart to the core of your stellar
life, and his lovely, lucid limbs will live as long
as you hold them up for the light that doesn't shine for men.

TRANSLATED BY LEWIS HYDE

Recent Poems

Los años

Son los años su peso o son su historia?
Lo que más cuesta es irse
despacio, aún con amor, sonriendo. Y dicen: "Joven;
ah, cuán joven estás..." ¿Estar, no ser? La lengua es justa.
Pasan esas figures sorprendentes. Porque el ojo—que está aún vivo—
    mira
y copia el oro del cabello, la carne rosa, el blanco del súbito marfil. La
    risa es clara
para todos, y también para él, que vive y óyela.
Pero los años echan
algo como una turbia claridad redonda,
y él marcha en el fanal odiado. Y no es visible
o apenas lo es, porque desconocido pasa, y sigue envuelto.
No es possible romper el vidrio o el aire
redondos, ese cono perpetuo que algo alberga:
aún un ser que se mueve y pasa, ya invisible.
Mientras los otros, libres, cruzan, ciegan.

Porque cegar es emitir su vida en rayos frescos.
Pero quien pasa a solas, protegido
por su edad, cruza sin ser sentido. El aire, inmóvil.
Él oye y siente, porque el muro extraño
roba a él la luz, pero aire es sólo
para la luz que llega, y pasa el filo.
Pasada el alma, en pie, cruza aún quien vive.

FROM *POEMAS DE LA CONSUMACIÓN*

The Years

Are the years a burden or are they a history?
What hurts the most is to walk off
slowly, still full of love, smiling. And they say: "Young;
ah, how young you look..." Look, not are? The language is precise.
Those fantastic shapes go by. Because the eye—it's still alive—watches
and reflects the gold of hair, the pink flesh, the white in a flash of ivory.
    The laugh is transparent
to anyone, including him; he lives and hears it.
But the years throw
something like a murky brightness around him,
and he walks in this lantern he despises. And he's not visible
or he barely is, because he goes by like a stranger and keeps going,
    shrouded.
It isn't possible to break the glass or the air
around him, that eternal cone sheltering something,
a person still who moves around and goes by, now invisible.
While the others, who are free, cross through and go blind.

Because to go blind is to give your life out as fresh rays of light.
But whoever goes alone, protected
by his age, crosses without being felt. The air does not move.
He hears and feels because the strange wall
strips him of light, but he is nothing but air
for the light that arrives, and he crosses the line.
The soul is long gone, yet someone alive is walking by.

Translated by Geoffrey Rips

Los viejos y los jóvenes

Unos, jóvenes, pasan. Ahí pasan, sucesivos,
ajenos a la tarde gloriosa que los unge.
Como esos viejos
más lentos van uncidos
a ese rayo final del sol poniente.
Éstos sí son conscientes de la tibieza de la tarde fina.
Delgado el sol les toca y ellos toman
su templanza: es un bien—¡quedan tan pocos!—,
y pasan despacioso por esa senda clara.

Es el verdor primero de la estacíon temprana.
Un río juvenil, más bien niñez de un manantial cercano,
y el verdor incipiente: robles tiernos,
bosque hacia el puerto en ascensión ligera.
Ligerísima. Mas no van ya los viejos a su ritmo.
Y allí los jóvenes que se adelantan pasan
sin ver, y siguen, sin mirarles.
Los ancianos los miran. Son estables,
éstos, los que al extremo de la vida,
en el borde del fin, quedan suspensos,
sin caer, cual por siempre.
Mientras las juveniles sombras pasan, ellos sí, consumibles, inestables,
urgidos de la sed que un soplo sacia.

FROM Poemas de la consumación

The Old and the Young

People walk by, young ones. There they go, one after another,
removed from the glorious evening that rubs them with its oil.
Like those old people
who move more slowly, harnessed
to the last ray of the sun in the west.
The old are well aware of the coolness of this clear evening.
The sun, thinned out, touches them and they take in
its mildness: it's a blessing—so few are left!—
and they move slowly along that bright path.

It is the early season's first flush of green.
The young river—more like the childhood of a nearby spring—
and the foliage about to break: tender oaks,
a forest rising lightly toward the mountain pass.
So lightly! But the old no longer move at that pace.
And over there, the young, taking the lead, go past them
without seeing, they move on and don't look back.
The old folks watch them. They're steady,
these people who, at the far side of life,
at the edge of the end, hang on
without falling, that way forever.
While the young shadows go past, so unstable, using themselves up,
driven by the thirst that one gust of air will satisfy.

TRANSLATED BY LEWIS HYDE

HORAS SESGAS

Durante algunos años fui diferente,

o fui el mismo. Evoqué principados, viles ejecutorias

o victoria sin par. Tristeza siempre.

Amé a quienes no quise. Y desamé a quien tuve.

Muralla fuera el mar, quizá puente ligero.

No sé si me conocí o si aprendí a ignorarme.

Si respeté a los peces, plata viva en las horas,

o intenté domeñar a la luz. Aquí palabras muertas.

Me levanté con enardecimiento, callé con sombra, y tarde.

Ávidamente ardí. Canté ceniza.

Y si metí en el agua un rostro no me reconocí. Narciso es triste.

Referí circunstancia. Imprequé a las esferas

y serví la materia de su música vana

con ademán intenso, sin saber si existía.

Entre las multitudes quise beber su sombra

como quien bebe el agua de un desierto engañoso.

Palmeras…Sí, yo canto…Pero nadie escuchaba.

Las dunas, las arenas palpitaban sin sueño.

Falaz escucho a veces una sombra corriendo

por un cuerpo creído. O escupo a solas. "Quémate."

Pero yo no me quemo. Dormir, dormir…¡Ah! "Acábate."

FROM *POEMAS DE LA CONSUMACIÓN*

BENT TIME

There were years when I was different
or the same. I invented principalities, horrible pedigrees
or a fantastic victory. Sadness all the time.
I loved people I didn't like. And I stopped loving the one I had.
The sea might have been a big wall, maybe a delicate bridge.
Did I know who I was or just learn to forget myself?
Did I honor the fish (lively silver in time)
or was I trying to domesticate light? Dead words here.
I got up hot with passion and fell quiet with shade, afternoon.
I burned greedily. I did the chant of ashes.
And when I looked into the water, I didn't know who I was. Narcissus
     is sad.
I reported the condition. I cursed the planets
and in my exaggerated style I served what comes
from their useless music, never sure if it was real.
I wanted to drink the shadow of crowds of people
like a man who drinks the water of a trick desert.
Palm trees... Yes, I'm singing... But no one used to listen.
The dunes, the sand used to throb without sleep.
Sometimes I hear a false shadow running
through what's supposed to be a body. Or I go off by myself and spit.
    "Burn yourself up."
But I'm not burning. Sleep, sleep... Yes! "Get it over with."

Translated by Lewis Hyde

Visión juvenil desde otros años

Al nacer se prodigan
las palabras que dicen muerte, asombro.
Como entre dos sonidos, hay un beso o un murmullo.
Conocer es reír, y el alba ríe.

Ríe, pues la tierra es un pecho que convulsivo late.
Carcajada total que no es son, pero vida,
pero luces que exhala
algo, un pecho: el planeta.

Es un cuerpo gozoso.
No importa lo que él lleva,
mas su inmenso latir por el espacio.
Como un niño flotando, como un niño en la dicha.
Así el joven miró y vio el mundo, libre.

Quizás entre dos besos,
quizá al seno de un beso:
Tal sintió entre dos labios.
Era un fresco reír, de él o del mundo.

Pero el mundo perdura,
no entre dos labios sólo: el beso acaba.
Pero el mundo rodando,
libre, sí, es cual un beso,
aún después que aquél muere.

From *Poemas de la consumación*

A Vision of Youth from Other Years

At birth words
are squandered saying death, terror.
As when between two sounds there is a kiss or a whisper.
To know is to laugh, and the dawn laughs.

It laughs, for the earth is a human chest beating convulsively.
A full laughter that isn't sound but life,
but lights exhaled by
something, a chest: the planet.

It is a joyful body.
What is on it doesn't matter.
Only its mammoth quivering in space.
Like a floating, happy child.
So the youth looked and saw the world, free.

Maybe between two kisses,
maybe at the heart of a kiss:
that's what he felt between two lips.
It was fresh laughter, his or the world's.

But the world endures,
not just between two lips: the kiss ends.
But the rolling world,
free, yes, is like a kiss
even after it dies.

TRANSLATED BY WILLIS BARNSTONE AND DAVID GARRISON

El cometa

La cabellera larga es algo triste.
Acaso dura menos
que las estrellas, si pensadas. Y huye.
Huye como el cometa.
Como el cometa "Haléy" cuando fui niño.
Un niño mira y cree.
Ve los cabellos largos
y mira, y ve la cauda
de un cometa que un niño izó hasta el cielo.

Pero el hombre ha dudado.
Ya puede él ver el cielo
surcado de fulgores.
Nunca creerá, y sonríe.
Sólo más tarde vuelve
a creer y ve sombras.
Desde sus blancos pelos ve negrores,
y cree. Todo lo ciego es ciego,
y él cree. Cree en el luto entero que él tentase.

Así niños y hombres
pasan. El hombre duda.
El viejo sabe. Sólo el niño conoce.
Todos miran correr la cola vívida.

FROM *Poemas de la consumación*

THE COMET

Its trailing hair is a little sad.
It must not last as long
as the stars, so thoughtful. And it flies off.
It flies off like the comet.
Like Halley's comet when I was a child.
A child watches and believes.
He sees the trailing tail
and what he sees are the holy robes
of a comet that was hoisted into the sky by a child.

But it's the grown-up who's skeptical.
Now he can see the sky
cut through with bright lights.
He'll never believe. He smiles.
Only later he believes
again. He sees shadows.
He can see black things inside his white hair,
and believes. He believes in all the black cloth that his fingers touched.

That's the way it is with children
and men. The man has his doubts.
The old man knows. Only the child understands.
They all watch the brilliant, circling tail.

TRANSLATED BY LEWIS HYDE

Si alguien me hubiera dicho

Si alguna vez pudieras
haberme dicho lo que no dijiste.
En esta noche casi perfecta, junto a la bóveda,
en esta noche fresca de verano.
Cuando la luna ha ardido;
quemóse la cuadriga; se hundió el astro.
Y en el cielo nocturno, cuajado de livideces huecas,
no hay sino dolor,
pues hay memoria, y soledad, y olvido.
Y hasta las hojas reflejadas caen. Se caen, y duran. Viven.

Si alguien me hubiera dicho.
No soy joven, y existo. Y esta mano se mueve.
Repta por esta sombra, explica sus venenos,
sus misteriosas dudas ante tu cuerpo vivo.
Hace mucho que el frío
cumplió años. La luna cayó en aguas.
El mar cerróse, y verdeció en sus brillos.
Hace mucho, muchísimo
que duerme. Las olas van calando.
Suena la espuma igual, sólo a silencio.
Es como un puño triste
y él agarra a los muertos y los explica,
y los sacude, y los golpea contra las rocas fieras.

Y los salpica. Porque los muertos, cuando golpeados,
cuando asestados contra el artero granito,
salpican. Son materia.
Y no hieden. Están aún más muertos,
y se esparcen y cubren, y no hacen ruido.

If Someone Could Have Told Me

If just once you'd told me the things you never said.
On this nearly perfect night, under the grave sky,
on this crisp summer night.
When the moon has burned;
the Charioteer eaten with his own fire; the star gone under.
And there's nothing but pain
in the night sky, spotted with pale holes,
because there's memory and loneliness and forgetfulness.
And even the reflected leaves are falling. They fall and endure. They live.

If someone could have told me.
I'm not young, and I exist. And this hand is moving.
It snakes through this dusk explaining its poison,
the mysterious doubt it has about your living body.
It's been some time since the cold
came of age. The moon fell in the water.
The sea closed up and turned a brilliant green.
It's been asleep for a long time,
a very long time. The waves are falling quiet.
The surf sounds the same: just silence.
It's like a sad fist
that grabs the dead and explains them,
it shakes them and beats them on the meat-eating rocks.

It spatters them about. Because when the dead are beaten,
when they're slapped against the cunning granite,
they spatter. They're material.
And they don't stink. They just get deader,
and they're scattered and spread around without a noise.

Son muertos acabados.

Quizás aún no empezados.
Algunos han amado. Otros hablaron mucho.
Y se explican. Inútil. Nadie escucha a los vivos.
Pero los muertos callan con más justos silencios.
Si tú me hubieras dicho.
Te conocí y he muerto.
Sólo falta que un puño,
un miserable puño me golpee,
me enarbole y me aseste,
y que mi voz se esparza.

FROM *POEMAS DE LA CONSUMACIÓN*

They're the done-for dead.

Maybe they haven't started yet.
Some were in love. Others talked a lot.
And they explained themselves. Silly. No one listens to the living.
But the silence of the dead is more fitting.
If you could have told me.
You were my friend and I've died.
I'm just waiting for a fist,
an insignificant fist to hit me,
to lift me up and swat me,
to scatter my voice.

TRANSLATED BY LEWIS HYDE

No lo conoce

La juventud no lo conoce, por eso dura, y sigue.
¿Adónde vais? Y sopla el viento, empuja
a los veloces que casi giran y van, van con el viento,
ligeros en el mar: pie sobre espuma.

Vida. Vida es ser joven y no más. Escucha,
escucha… Pero el callado son
no se denuncia
sino sobre los labios de los jóvenes.
En el beso lo oyen. Sólo ellos,
en su delgado oír,
pueden, o escuchan.
Roja pulpa besada que pronuncian.

FROM *POEMAS DE LA CONSUMACIÓN*

Doesn't Know

Youth doesn't know, that's why it goes on, endures.
Where are you going? And the wind blows, pushes
the runners who almost spin and go, go with the wind,
graceful on the sea: foot over foam.

Life. Life is to be young and nothing else. Listen,
listen … But the hushed sound
doesn't betray itself
except on the lips of the young.
They hear it in the kiss. Only they,
with their sharp hearing
catch it, or listen.
Red-kissed pulp which they enunciate.

Translated by David Garrison

LLUEVE

En esta tarde llueve, y llueve pura
tu imagen. En mi recuerdo el día se abre. Entraste.
No oigo. La memoria me da tu imagen sólo.
Sólo tu beso o lluvia cae en recuerdo.
Llueve tu voz, y llueve el beso triste,
el beso hondo,
beso mojado en lluvia. El labio es húmedo.
Húmedo de recuerdo el beso llora
desde unos cielos grises
delicados.
Llueve tu amor mojando mi memoria,
y cae, cae. El beso
al hondo cae. Y gris aún cae
la lluvia.

FROM *POEMAS DE LA CONSUMACIÓN*

It's Raining

This evening it's raining, and my picture of you is raining.
The day falls open in my memory. You walked in.
I can't hear. Memory gives me nothing but your picture.
There only your kiss or the rain is falling.
Your voice is raining, your sad kiss is raining,
the deep kiss,
the kiss soaked with rain. Lips are moist.
Moist with its memories the kiss weeps
from some delicate
gray heavens.
Rain falls from your love, dampening my memory,
keeps on falling. The kiss
falls far down. The gray rain
goes on falling.

Translated by Robert Bly

CERCANO A LA MUERTE

No es la tristeza lo que la vida arrumba
o acerca, cuando los pasos muchos son, y duran.
Allá el monte, aquí la vidriada ciudad,
o es un reflejo de ese sol larguísimo
que urde respuestas
a distancia
para los labios que, viviendo, viven,
o recuerdan.
La majestad de la memoria es aire
después, o antes. Los hechos son suspiro.
Ese telón de sedas amarillas
que un soplo empuja, y otra luz apaga.

FROM *POEMAS DE LA CONSUMACIÓN*

CLOSE TO DEATH

It isn't sadness that life piles up or brings forward when the passings
  are so many and go on so long.
The mountain over there and here the glassy city,
or a reflection of the drawn-out sun
that fabricates answers
from a distance
for the living lips that live
or have memories.
The wonder of memory is air
when it's over, or before. What was done is a sigh.
That yellow silk curtain, pushed
by a breath of wind, extinguished by some other light.

TRANSLATED BY LEWIS HYDE

El límite

Basta. No es insistir mirar el brillo largo
de tus ojos. Allí, hasta el fin del mundo.
Miré y obtuve. Contemplé, y pasaba.
La dignidad del hombre está en su muerte.
Pero los brillos temporales ponen
color, verdad. La luz pensada engaña.
Basta. En el caudal de luz—tus ojos—puse
mi fe. Por ellos vi, viviera.
Hoy que piso mi fin, beso estos bordes.
Tú, mi limitación, mi sueño. ¡Seas!

FROM *POEMAS DE LA CONSUMACIÓN*

The Limit

Enough. It isn't that I need to keep looking at the full light
of your eyes. There, till the end of the world.
I looked and got what I wanted. I thought about it and it was happening.
Man's dignity is in his death.
But the brightness in the world brings out
color, truth. The light in the mind is deceptive.
Enough. I put my faith in the storehouse of light—
your eyes. Because of them I saw and lived.
Today as I walk my last, I kiss these borders.
You, my limitation, my dream. You live!

TRANSLATED BY GEOFFREY RIPS

El olvido

No es tu final como una copa vana
que hay que apurar. Arroja el casco, y muere.

Por eso lentamente levantas en tu mano
un brillo o su mención, y arden tus dedos,
como una nieve súbita.
Está y no estuvo, pero estuvo y calla.
El frío quema y en tus ojos nace
su memoria. Recordar es obsceno;
peor: es triste. Olvidar es morir.

Con dignidad murió. Su sombra cruza.

FROM *POEMAS DE LA CONSUMACIÓN*

What Is Forgotten

Your end isn't like a worthless cup
that must be drained. Throw away the empty and die.

Therefore you slowly lift a brightness
in your hand or some mention of it, and your fingers burn,
like a sudden snowfall.
It is and was not, but it used to be and is silent.
The cold burns and its memory comes to life
in your eyes. It's obscene to remember;
worse: it's sad. To forget is to die.

He died with dignity. His shadow crosses over.

Translated by Geoffrey Rips

Como Moisés es el viejo

Como Moisés en lo alto del monte.

Cada hombre puede ser aquél
y mover la palabra y alzar los brazos
y sentir como barre la luz, de su rostro,
el polvo viejo de los caminos.

Porque allí está la puesta.
Mira hacia atrás: el alba.
Adelante: más sombras. ¡Y apuntaban las luces!
Y él agita los brazos y proclama la vida,
desde su muerte a solas.

Porque como Moisés, muere.
No con las tablas vanas y el punzón, y el rayo en las alturas,
sino rotos los textos en la tierra, ardidos
los cabellos, quemados los oídos por las palabras terribles,
y aún aliento en los ojos, y en el pulmón la llama,

y en la boca la luz.
Para morir basta un ocaso.
Una porción de sombra en la raya del horizonte.
Un hormiguear de juventudes, esperanzas, voces.
Y allá la sucesión, la tierra: el límite.
Lo que verán los otros.

FROM *Poemas de la consumación*

The Old Man Is Like Moses

Like Moses on top of the mountain.

Every man can be like that
and deliver the word and lift up his arms
and feel how the light sweeps
the old road dust from his face.

Because the sunset is over there.
Looking behind him: the dawn.
In front: the growing shadows. And the lights began to shine!
And he swings his arms and speaks for the living
from inside his own death, all alone.

Because like Moses, he dies.
Not with the useless tablets and the chisel and the lightning in the
    mountains
but with words broken on the ground, his hair
on fire, his ears singed by the terrifying words.
And the breath is still in his eyes and the spark in his lungs
and his mouth full of light.

A sunset is sufficient for death.
A serving of shadow on the edge of the horizon.
A swarming of youth and hope and voices.
And in that place the generations to come, the earth: the borderline.
The thing the others will see.

TRANSLATED BY LEWIS HYDE

Sonido de la guerra

El soldado

Aquí llegué. Aquí me quedo. Es triste
saber que el día en noche encarna. Eterna
mire la luz en unos ojos bellos.
¡Cuán lejos ya! Aquí en la selva acato
la única luz, y vivo. Pues ignoro
aquí de dónde vengo. Son las aves
tenaces las que sobreviven, las que
sobrevuelan. Aquí a mis pies lianas
bullen, y sienten que tierra es todo, y nada
es diferente. El cielo no es distinto.
El ave es tierra y vuela.
Lo mismo garza que alcotán. ¡Qué pájaros
fantasmas! El agua pasa y cunde.
Aquí mi cuerpo mineral hoy puede
vivir. Soy piedra pues que existo.

El brujo

Solo quedé. Arrasada está la aldea.
Ah, el miserable
conquistador pasó. Metralla y, más, veneno
vi en la mirada horrible. Y eran jóvenes.
Cuántas veces soñé con un suspiro
como una muerte dulce. En mis brebajes
puse el beleño de no ser, y supe
dormir, terrible ciencia última.
Mas hoy no me valió. Con ojo fijo

Sound of the War

The Soldier

I made it here. Here I'll stay. It's a sad thing
knowing that day is embodied in night. I looked
at the changeless light in some pretty eyes.
So far away now! While I'm in this forest I accept
its only light, and live. I really don't know
where I came from. Only tireless birds
survive, those that fly over.
Vines swarm at my feet here,
feeling that earth is all there is,
and everything's alike. The sky's no different.
The bird is earth and it soars.
Heron and falcon, one and the same.
What shadowy birds, what shrieking
shadows! The water flows and spreads.
My mineral body can live here
today. I'm stone because I exist.

The Sorcerer

Only I survived. The village was destroyed.
Oh, that hateful
conqueror came this way. I saw shrapnel, even poison
in his wicked eyes. And they were so young.
I dreamt so often of a sigh
as sweet as death. I put the henbane
of nonbeing in my potions, and I discovered
sleep, that terrible last art.
But today it failed me. Without flinching

velé y mire, y seco
un ojo vio la lluvia, y era roja.
Pálido y seco,
y ensangrentado en su interior, cegó.

El soldado

No estoy dormido. No sé si muero o sueño.
En esta herida está el vivir, y ya
tan sólo ella es la vida.
Tuve unos labios que significaron.
Un cuerpo que se erguía, un brazo extenso,
como unas manos que aprehendieron: cosas,
objetos, seres, esperanzas, humos.
Soñé, y la mano dibujaba el sueño,
el deseo. Tenté. Quien tienta vive. Quien conoce ha muerto.
Sólo mi pensamiento vive ahora.
Por eso muero. Porque ya no miro,
pero sé. Joven lo fui. Y sin edad, termino.

El brujo

Pues vi, miré. La sangre no era un río,
sino su pensamiento doloroso.
La sangre vive cuando presa pugna
por surtir. Pero si surte, muere.
Como un castillo donde prisionera
está la bella y un dulce caballero
abre el portón, y sale: la luz mata.
Así la sangre, en que el destino yerra,
pues si fulgura muere. Ah, qué misterio
increíble. Sólo sobre unos labios coloridos,
como tras celosía, se adivina

I stood and watched, and my dry eye
saw that the rain was red.
Pale and dry,
bloodied on the inside, it went blind.

The Soldier

I'm not asleep. I don't know if I'm dying or dreaming.
Life is inside this wound, and now
this wound alone is life.
My lips had meaning.
I had a body that stood up, a long arm,
like some hands that grabbed: things,
objects, people, expectations, smoke.
I dreamt, and my hand sketched the dream,
the desire. I touched. Whoever touches lives. Whoever knows has died.
Only my thoughts are still alive.
That's why I'm dying. Because I no longer look,
but I know. Once I was young. Ageless, I reach the end.

The Sorcerer

I saw, I looked. The blood wasn't a river,
it was only the painful image of itself.
The blood lives when, captured, it struggles
to spurt out. But if it spurts, it dies.
Like a castle where a beautiful woman
is held prisoner, and a kindhearted knight pushes
the heavy door open, and she steps out: the light kills.
Just as the blood, where destiny wanders about,
would die if it flashed. What an incredible
mystery! Only on some painted lips,
as if behind a lattice, can you make out

el bulto de la sangre. Y el amante
puede besar y presentir, ¡sin verla!

El pájaro

¿Quién habla aquí en la noche? Son venenos
humanos. Soy ya viejo y oigo poco,
mas no confundo el canto de la alondra
con el ronco trajín del pecho pobre.
Miro y en torno casi ya no hay aire
para mis alas. Ni rama para mi descanso.
¿Qué subversion pasó? Nada conozco.
Naturaleza huyó. ¿Qué es esto? Y vuelo
en un aire que mata.
Letal ceniza en que bogar, y muero.

El soldado

Qué sed horrible. En tierra seca, nada.
Tendido estoy y sólo veo estrellas.
El agujero de mi pecho alienta
como brutal error. Pienso, no hablo.
Siento. Alguna vez sentir fuera vivir.
Quizás hoy siento porque estoy muriendo.
Y la postrer palabra sea: Sentí.

El brujo

Camino a tientas. ¿Entre piedras ando
o entre miembros dispersos? ¿Frío un talon o es una frente rota?
Qué rumoroso un trozo que está solo:
Más allá de la muerte vive algo,
un resto, en vida propia. Y ando, aparto
esa otra vida a solas que no entiendo.

256

the shape of the blood. And the lover
can kiss and imagine, without seeing her!

The Bird

Who's chattering at this time of night? Some human
poison… I'm old and don't hear too well anymore,
but I couldn't confuse the lark's song
with the hoarse working of poor souls.
I look around, but there's hardly any air left
for my wings. Nor a branch for me to rest on.
What mixed things up? Nothing's familiar.
Nature fled. What's this? And I fly
on air that kills.
Deadly ashes for rowing, and I'm dying.

The Soldier

What a terrible thirst. On dry land, nothing.
I'm lying down and all I can see is the stars.
The hole in my chest breathes
like a stupid mistake. I think, I don't speak.
I feel. At one time feeling was living.
Maybe I can feel today because I'm dying.
And my last words will be: I felt.

The Sorcerer

I'm groping in the dark. Am I walking among rocks
or scattered limbs? Is this cold thing a claw or a broken face?
A cut-off fragment makes a lot of noise:
Something is stirring beyond death,
a leftover chunk, with a life of its own. I go on, pushing aside
that other isolated life I can't understand.

El soldado

Si alguien llegase… No puedo hablar. No
puedo gritar. Fui joven y miraba, ardía,
tocaba, sonaba. El hombre suena. Pero mudo, muero.
Y aquí y a las estrellas se apagaron,
pues que mis ojos y alas desconocen.
Sólo el aire del pecho suena. El estertor
dentro de mí respire por la herida,
como por una boca. Boca inútil.
Reciente, y hecha sólo
para morir.

El brujo

La guerra fue porque está siendo. Yerran
los que la nombran. Nada valen y son sólo palabras
las que te arrastran, sombra polvorosa,
humo estallado, humano que resultas
como una idea muerta tras su nada
¿Dónde el beleño de tu sueño, zumo
para dormir, si todo ha muerto y veo
sólo que la luz piensa? No, no hay vida,
sino este pensamiento en que yo acabo:
El pensamiento de la luz sin hombres.

La alondra

Todo está quieto y todo está desierto.
Y el alba nace, y muda.
Pasé como una piedra y fui a la mar.

FROM *DIÁLOGOS DEL CONOCIMIENTO*

The Soldier

If someone came… I can't talk.
I can't cry out. I was young, I was awake, aroused,
I touched and made noise. Man makes noise. But if I don't speak, I die.
And the stars have already burned out here,
since my eyes can no longer recognize them.
Only the air in my chest makes any noise. The death rattle
in me breathes through my wound,
as if it were a mouth. A useless mouth.
New, and made only for dying.

The Sorcerer

There was war because it continues. Those that name it
are making a mistake. They're worthless and they're only words
that drag you down, dusty shadow,
exploded smoke, man who is
like an idea dead behind nothingness.
Where's the henbane of your dream, potion
for sleeping, if everything has died and I see
nothing, but light that thinks? No, there's no life,
only this thought in which I'm disappearing:
The thought of light without people.

The Lark

Everything's still, deserted.
The sun rises and can't speak.
I flew by like a stone and headed toward the sea.

TRANSLATED BY DAVID UNGER

Descriptive Bibliography

(Note: Aleixandre's own comments on each book, taken from the brief prefaces he wrote for Spanish anthologies, appear here in quotation marks.)

Ámbito (in English: *Ambit* or *Surroundings*). Written between 1924 and 1927.

Although some of Aleixandre's later themes can be found if the book is read with them in mind, *Surroundings* is, for the most part, traditional in both approach and form, as much influenced by classical and baroque formalism as by any of the modernists.

Pasión de la tierra (*The Earth's Passion*). Written between 1928 and 1929. Originally announced under the title *La evasión hacia el fondo* (*The Escape to the Depths*).

Twenty-one prose poems written in an almost hermetic dream-language, the book serves as a breeding ground for the work that follows. It is like the vision a young man has that neither he nor his elders can fully understand, but which he nonetheless records and then goes on to clarify. Here is the raw material, all in a heap.

"This book... is poetry 'as it is born,' with a minimum of elaboration. It was some time later that I realized, though I was unaware of it at the time, how much this book owes to my reading of a psychologist (Freud) whose influence on literature has been vast, and whom I had just come to know in those same years.

"*The Earth's Passion*, because of the technique it uses, is the book of mine that is hardest to read. I have always thought I could see in its chasm-like layers the sudden start of my poetry's evolution, which, from its earliest, has been—I have said—a longing for the light. This book has therefore produced in me a double, complicated feeling: of aversion, because of its difficulty, which contradicts the call, the appeal it makes to basic levels, common to all of us; and of affection, for the maternal humus out of which it grew."

Espadas como labios (*Swords like Lips*). Written between 1930 and 1931.

Aleixandre returns to verse poems in this book, but now he is clearly at work in a surrealist vein. The poems are marked by odd turns of phrase, syntactic inversions, and private imagery. The shorter poems, in particular, though written in an elegant and metrical line, are as restrained and obscure as the poems of *The Earth's Passion.* The longer poems, like "The Waltz," move about with a more playful and accessible sureality.

La destrucción o el amor (*Destruction or Love*). Written between 1932 and 1933.

Finished in less than a year, in a burst of energy after a period of convalescence (during which Aleixandre did not write at all—"Health: creativity. They are the same to me... In this I am a complete anti-romantic."), the book reveals a vision of a violent, instinctual world whose one constant is an eroticism at once unifying and destructive.

"I believe that the poet's vision of the world reaches its first fullness with this work, conceived out of the central idea of the amorous unity of the universe."

This is Aleixandre's finest early work; both the vision and the style are clearly and distinctively his own. It won him the *Premio nacional de literatura.*

Mundo a solas (*The World by Itself*). Written between 1934 and 1936, but not published until 1950.

"This book, perhaps the poet's most pessimistic..., sings of man as debased, set apart from his primitive elementality; it sings of the dawn of the universe now far away and extinguished... Man is a shadow; 'man doesn't exist.'"

Sombra del paraíso (*The Shadow of Paradise*). Written between 1939 and 1943.

"The principal theme, that of a paradise, is laid out, on the one hand, through a vision of the cosmos in its glory before man appeared and, with his appearance, a vision of sorrow and limitation. (See the seven poems of the series 'The Immortals.') This central nucleus is filled out, on the other hand..., with the poems that address themselves to man as a perishable creature, from the knowledge of his transitoriness and a concern for his destiny ('What Happens to All Flesh,'... and some others). This level anticipates the concern with human life whose central development had to await a later work, *The Story of the Heart*."

The book continues Aleixandre's creation myth, but turns as well to more temporal themes (his childhood in particular). Much of the imagery for "paradise" is drawn from the seacoast around Málaga where Aleixandre lived as a boy. "Without that city, without that Andalusian shore where my entire childhood was spent and whose light was to remain indelibly in my eyes, this book—which... can justly be called Mediterranean—would never have existed..."

Nacimiento último (*Final Birth*). Though the book contains a few very early poems, the bulk was written between 1944 and 1952.

The only work of Aleixandre's "that doesn't form a self-contained organism." There are three discrete sections. The first, bearing the same title as the book itself, is structured around the idea of "death [as] amorous destruction and a reintegration into unity, in that sense, a true 'final birth.'" The second section consists of verse sketches and homages to various people, while the last group is a series of "paradise poems" written as a continuation of *The Shadow of Paradise*.

Historia del corazón (*The History*... or *The Story of the Heart*).
Written between 1945 and 1953.

"*The Story of the Heart* presumed... a new view, a new conception
in the poet's spirit. The central theme, living a human life, is sung here
as it flows from two different springs: a vision of man as he lives, from
the awareness of his temporality (poems, therefore, about human age:
about childhood, youth, maturity, old age); and a vision of love as the
transcendent symbol of man's solidarity before 'the terms' of his life. The
terms... and *the* term, whose semblance hovers over the whole book. Its
composition was begun as a work of love in the strict sense, but the intu-
ition quickly opened and enlarged to make room for a fuller vision and
grasp."

En un vasto dominio (*In a Spacious Kingdom*). Written between 1958
and 1962.

The first part of the book invokes "human material," a sort of vol-
canic magma which rose out of the earth and took on life. It is cata-
logued in a series of poems on parts of the body ("The Belly," "The
Arm," "Blood," "Sex"). This is the most spacious of kingdoms, matter
enlivened with spirit.

"In the last part of *The Shadow of Paradise* and in *The Story of the
Heart,* the poet... reflected on human temporality—in the individual
and in the collective. Here he turns to face life in history since the very
beginning of the originating material. There is only one material, in the
view of the poet, and it grows step by step until it emerges, through a
spiritualized process, with the arrival of man. The intent of the first
'chapter'... is to write a minutely detailed history of the human body
rising up out of that originating material. This material was made life
and life becomes history."

Retratos con nombre (*Titled Portraits*). Written between 1958 and
1964.

Poems about, dedicated to, or inspired by various people: Jorge

Guillén, Rafael Alberti, Dámaso Alonso, Paul Eluard, Max Aub, and many more (including Aleixandre's dog). The title is in opposition to the last section of *In a Spacious Kingdom,* a series of "Anonymous Portraits."

Poemas de la consumación (*Poems at the End* or *The Poems of Ripeness*). Written between 1965 and 1966.

A book of spare, thoughtful poems in which, instead of the equation "Love equals Death," now "Wisdom equals Death." The old man finds that age has brought him knowledge, but—though mental life has its own, cool beauty—the real life, the juice of life, is in discovery and activity.

"This book... attempts... to sing about the situation of the old man who lives fully aware that life really lies with youth. The rest is shadow, forgotten. It is not an elegaic book, but it may be a tragic one (as someone has called it). And what is inexorable in the end [in *la consumación*] one takes on as a knowledge that has a value of its own, a clouded illumination, I might say.

"In this book I felt it necessary to use irrational elements in the poems, but without having this entail an unnecessary return to those forms of expression already used in my surrealist stage. I tried, therefore, to irrationalize the expressive element 'out of' the experience of realism, if I may use that imprecise word, of my [recent] books..."

Diálogos del conocimiento (*Dialogues of Knowledge*). Written between 1966 and 1973.

A book of complicated, intellectual poems. In each "dialogue" we hear two voices—a ballet dancer and a choreographer, a soldier and a sorcerer, two young poets, and so on (even two different voices in the head of Marcel Proust). But though there are always two voices, there is no real dialogue. The speakers only obliquely influence each other.

"Reality... is much too rich, since its content can become evident from only one perspective and, as such, ends up being wholly personal, leaving out the countless panoramas that only other points of view could offer. This is the idea that led me to cast my book... in a dramatic form. I wanted to create a series of characters who were distinct from the author and different also among themselves, who would serve me as perspectives or agencies of knowledge, out of whose biases a multiplicity, like that of the universe, might be presented. Most of the dialogues are not dialogues at all, but rather plaited monologues; the dialogue takes place inside the reader."

ORIGINAL EDITIONS OF THE POETRY

Ámbito (Litoral, Málaga: 1928)

Pasión de la tierra (Fábula, Mexico City: 1935)

Espadas como labios (Espasa Calpe, Madrid: 1932)

La destrucción o el amor (Signo, Madrid: 1935)

Mundo a solas (Clan, Madrid: 1950)

Sombra del paraíso (Adán, Madrid: 1944)

Nacimiento último (Insula, Madrid: 1953)

Historia del corazón (Espasa Calpe, Madrid: 1954)

En un vasto dominio (Revista de Occidente, Madrid: 1962)

Retratos con nombre (El Bardo, Barcelona: 1965)

Poemas de la consumación (Plaza & Janés, Barcelona: 1968)

Diálogos del conocimiento (Plaza & Janés, Barcelona: 1974)

Indexes

Index of Titles (Spanish)

Index of Titles (English)

Index of First Lines (Spanish)

Index of First Lines (English)

Index of Translators

In addition to his work as a translator and editor, LEWIS HYDE is a poet and cultural critic with a particular interest in the public life of the imagination. His 1983 book *The Gift: Imagination and the Erotic Life of Property* illuminates and defends the noncommercial portion of artistic practice. *Trickster Makes This World: Mischief, Myth, and Art* (1998) uses a group of ancient myths to argue for the kind of disruptive intelligence all cultures need if they are to remain lively, flexible, and open to change. A MacArthur Fellow and former director of undergraduate creative writing at Harvard University, Hyde teaches during the fall semesters at Kenyon College, where he is the Richard L. Thomas Professor of Creative Writing. During the rest of the year, he lives in Cambridge, Massachusetts, writing.

The Chinese character for poetry is made up of two parts: "word" and "temple." It also serves as pressmark for Copper Canyon Press.

Since 1972, Copper Canyon Press has fostered the work of emerging, established, and world-renowned poets for an expanding audience. The Press thrives with the generous patronage of readers, writers, booksellers, librarians, teachers, students, and funders—everyone who shares the belief that poetry is vital to language and living.

Major funding has been provided by:
Anonymous
The Paul G. Allen Family Foundation
Lannan Foundation
National Endowment for the Arts
Washington State Arts Commission

For information and catalogs:
COPPER CANYON PRESS
Post Office Box 271
Port Townsend, Washington 98368
360-385-4925
www.coppercanyonpress.org

Printed in the USA
CPSIA information can be obtained
at www.ICGtesting.com
JSHW022211140824
68134JS00018B/990